**Friend of
the Library Donor**

Selected for the readers of
Lincoln City by
PATTY HERINGER, librarian,
1976-1998

A Complete Guide to
Making & Designing Today's Hats

Classic Millinery Techniques

Ann Albrizio

Coauthored & Illustrated by Osnat Lustig

Photographs by Ted Morrison

Lark Books

Editor: Dawn Cusick
Art/Production: Elaine Thompson
Photographer: Ted Morrison
Photographic Assistance: Coco Lee Thuman, Producer;
    Manfred Koh C. Hong, Assistant
Production Assistance: Hannes Charen, Bobby Gold
Editorial Assistance: Evans Carter

Photographs on pages 41, 43, 44, 118, and 130 by ok! Studio;
    all others copyright Ted Morrison.

Library of Congress Cataloging-in-Publication Data
Available

10 9 8 7 6 5 4 3 2 1

First Edition

Published by Lark Books
50 College St.
Asheville, NC 28801, US

© 1998, Ann Albrizio and Osnat Lustig

Distributed by Random House, Inc.,
    in the United States, Canada, the United Kingdom, Europe, and Asia

Distributed in Australia by Capricorn Link (Australia) Pty Ltd.,
    P.O. Box 6651, Baulkham Hills Business Centre, NSW 2153, Australia

Distributed in New Zealand by Tandem Press Ltd.,
    2 Rugby Rd., Birkenhead, Auckland, New Zealand

Printed in Hong Kong

All rights reserved

ISBN 1-57990-016-x

DEDICATION

This book is dedicated to the memory of my late husband James H. Orvin
whose love and support were constant during my long career
as a millinery professional and educator.

ACKNOWLEDGEMENT

Throughout my career I met many wonderful people who encouraged and cheered me, and I wish to thank them all. Extra special to me were my two uncles—the late Conrad Albrizio who was a gifted painter and the late Humberd Albrizio whose murals adorned the University of Louisiana for many years. These two men were a source of inspiration and creativity for years to come. With special acknowledgement to Marie Scarra, my sister, my best friend, and my business partner, thank you for being there for me through thick and thin; to my friend Osnat Lustig who helped me bring this book to life; to Rob Pulleyn and the Lark team for publishing this book, thus giving me one more way to share my passion for hats; but above and beyond, to all my students, both current and former, who through the years became such great ambassadors to classic millinery techniques.

Ann Albrizio
New York, New York

"Don't worry about price; worry about quality."
—Uncle Humberd

My many thanks to Ann Albrizio for her friendship and trust, for sharing with me the myriad facets of millinery, and for all the times she would say: "You know, there is another method of doing that…"; to Dawn Cusick for being such an urbane editor and guiding me in the right direction; to Lark's publisher, Rob Pulleyn, who just knew that Ann's millinery techniques need to be known to all; to Ted Morrison, CoCo, Manfred, and Flo for making the photographs come alive; to Jay Dershowitz of Dersh Feathers for sharing his vast knowledge and feather treasures; to Robert Baensch for opening my eyes; to Ken Coleman, my partner; and to all of Ann's students who loaned hats for the book's photo gallery and whose works show just what can be accomplished when combining imagination with classic millinery techniques.

Osnat Lustig
New York, New York

"Where are you planning to put all these hats?!"
—Ken Coleman

CONTENTS

Introduction 7

Gallery 40

Getting Started
Materials & Equipment 41
Basic Stitches 46
Choosing and Handling Fabric 47
Measuring the Head 48
Useful Practices 49
Proportion & Balance 50
Millinery Ribbons 50

Soft Hats
The Shirred Beret 54
The Two-Section Beret 57
The Stylized Beret 60
The Multi-Section Beret 66
The Visor 69
The Cloche 172

Rigid Frame Hats
The Pillbox 80
The Boater 83
Covering a Boater Frame with Straw Braid 86
Designing and Covering Rigid Frames . . . 88
Simple Blocked Crowns for Covered Frames 92

Turbans
The Basic Turban 95
The Built-Up Turban 98

Special Occasion Hats

The Cocktail Hat 102
Keeping Hats On 104
The Garland 107

Trimmings

Ribbons & Bows 109
Rosettes 111
Veils 112
Horsehair Brims 112
Dyeing Silk Flowers 114

Feathers

Millinery Feathers 116
Feather-Pads Hat 119
One-by-One Feather Hat 120
Feather Trims 122

Beyond Basics

The Millinery Workroom 126
Starting a Small Millinery Business . . . 127

Appendixes

The Millinery Ruler 129
Headsize Plates 130
Pressing Roll 132
French Curve 133

Glossary 134

Sources 138

Suggested Reading 141

Index 142

INTRODUCTION

Dear Reader,

This book is based on Basic Millinery, the first of five courses in the curriculum I designed for the Millinery Certificate program at The Fashion Institute of Technology in New York City. My experience in teaching millinery for over twenty years at FIT, combined with questions, problems, and successes of my many students, were the basis to the way processes are explained, the order of the hats, and the various hints throughout the book.

Many of the hats pictured in this book were made by my students. They have learned how to design their own patterns and to create unique hats. With the detailed instructions that follow, you, too, will be able to design and make professional quality hats. Make the most out of this book by following these important steps:

- First, it is important to read each chapter completely before cutting the fabric.

- Second, have all the necessary materials and tools ready before you start working. There are few things more frustrating than to be totally involved in a new hat and suddenly realizing that you don't have buckram on hand.

- Finally, use common sense and try to develop an eye for putting together colors, patterns, and lines that will flatter face and figure.

The chapters are arranged in increasing complexity, so if you have never made hats before, start from the very beginning. Even more experienced milliners will find new techniques and tips to add to their toolbox. Once you start making hats you will notice them everywhere: in old movies, in flea markets, in the most avant-garde fashion settings. Make notes to yourself about materials, design, and color. Above all, keep making and wearing hats!

Ann Albrizio

GALLERY

THE HATS IN THIS GALLERY WERE ALL MADE USING THE MILLINERY TECHNIQUES IN THIS BOOK. THEIR CREATORS HAVE ADDED FUN TWISTS SUCH AS LACING, ZIPPERS, REVERSIBLE DESIGNS, AND ASYMMETRICAL SHAPES, TO MENTION JUST A FEW, TO THE TO THE BASIC TECHNIQUES. WHEN SEEKING INSPIRATION FOR YOUR NEXT HAT DESIGN, JUST OBSERVE YOUR SURROUNDINGS. SHAPES AND TEXTURES OF THINGS LIKE A CAKE, A DRESS, A BOUQUET OF FLOWERS, A CLOUD IN THE SKY, A PIECE OF JEWELRY, OR A WINDOW DRESSING OFFER INSTANT SEEDS OF IDEAS. THE HATS SHOWN HERE REPRESENT JUST A SMALL SAMPLING OF INNUMERABLE POSSIBILITIES... WON'T YOU GIVE IT A TRY?

SHIRRED BERET

A SHIRRED BERET MADE FROM A PRINTED BRUSHED KNIT AND TRIMMED WITH A WIRED RIBBON HEAD-
BAND AND BOW; MILLI FINESTEIN, MILLINER.

BOATERS

LEFT: A BOATER COVERED WITH A NARROW BLUE STRAW BRAID AND TRIMMED WITH A WIDE STRAW BRAID BOW; OSNAT LUSTIG, MILLINER. *RIGHT:* A BOATER COVERED WITH A WIDE PALE GREEN ONION STRAW BRAID AND TRIMMED WITH A PEACH-TONE VEILING STRIP TIED TO A BOW; ANN ALBRIZIO, MILLINER.

TWO-SECTION BERETS

LEFT: A TWO-SECTION BERET MADE FROM A FLANNEL PLAID WITH A FRINGE AND PIN TRIM; MILLI FINESTEIN, MILLINER. *CENTER:* A TWO-SECTION BERET MADE FROM A MANMADE RED FUR WITH A BLACK HEADBAND; MARGARET PATTERSON, MILLINER. *RIGHT:* A TWO-SECTION BERET MADE FROM A RAW SILK PLAID TRIMMED WITH WIRED SELF-FABRIC BOW; OSNAT LUSTIG, MILLINER.

STYLIZED BERETS

LEFT: A STYLIZED BERET, PAGODA STYLE, MADE FROM A BLACK/MULTI LINEN PRINT; OSNAT LUSTIG, MILLINER. *CENTER:* A STYLIZED BERET, PAGODA STYLE, MADE FROM A CHINESE-INFLUENCED RED SATIN PRINT; JEAN SMITH, MILLINER. *RIGHT:* A FOUR-SECTION STYLIZED BERET MADE FROM A GOLD AND GREEN JACQUARD TRIMMED WITH TAILORED, SELF-FABRIC BOWS; KENNETH PHILLIPS, MILLINER.

BASIC TURBANS

LEFT: AN ASYMMETRIC TURBAN, MADE FROM BURGUNDY VELVET AND TRIMMED WITH A BURNT OSTRICH PLUME; ANN ALBRIZIO, MILLINER. *CENTER:* SIMPLE TURBAN MADE FROM A BLACK AND WHITE PRINTED COTTON AND TRIMMED WITH WIRED, SELF-FABRIC LOOPS; JUDITH TOBIAS, MILLINER. *RIGHT:* SIMPLE TURBAN MADE FROM A MULTICOLOR CREPE DE CHINE SILK WITH A STRAW CLOTH VISOR; OSNAT LUSTIG, MILLINER.

BUILT-UP TURBANS

LEFT: TURBAN WITH A KERCHIEF EXTENSION MADE FROM A FUCHSIA VELVETEEN EMBELLISHED WITH SEWN-ON BLACK SEQUINS; ANN ALBRIZIO, MILLINER. *RIGHT:* TURBAN WITH A SINGLE CRESCENT TIER MADE FROM A MULTICOLOR BRUSHED KNIT; OSNAT LUSTIG, MILLINER.

PILLBOXES

LEFT: PILLBOX MADE FROM A SILVER AND BLACK BROCADE OVER A BUCKRAM FOUNDATION AND TRIMMED WITH A LARGE SELF-FABRIC, MULTI-LOOP BOW; JULIANA KALOO, MILLINER. *CENTER:* PILLBOX MADE FROM A PRINTED BROCADE OVER A SOFT FLEXIE FOUNDATION; OSNAT LUSTIG, MILLINER. *RIGHT:* PILLBOX MADE FROM A WHITE BROCADE OVER A BUCKRAM FOUNDATION TRIMMED WITH PEARLS AND BEADS; KENNETH PHILLIPS, MILLINER.

PILLBOXES

LEFT: Pillbox made from a purple wool knit trimmed with a black tassel; Arthur Banner, milliner. *CENTER:* Pillbox made from red linen strips trimmed with a plaid ribbon cockade; Osnat Lustig, milliner. *RIGHT:* Hat and trim made from a single piece of gold and black lamé with the excess fabric gathered to form a bow-like trim; Ann Albrizio, milliner.

FEATHER BRIDAL HEADPIECE

BRIDAL HEADPIECE MADE FROM A FOUNDATION OF WHITE WOOL FELT COVERED WITH INDIVIDUAL WHITE
GOOSE COQUILLE FEATHERS AND TRIMMED WITH CURLED FEATHER FLOWERS; OSNAT LUSTIG, MILLINER.

LEFT: CLOCHE MADE FROM A JEWEL-TONE BROCADE WITH A SELF-FABRIC COVERED BUTTON TRIM; JEAN SMITH, MILLINER. *CENTER:* REVERSIBLE CLOCHE WITH A SOFT PILLBOX-STYLE CROWN MADE FROM FLORAL COTTON ON ONE SIDE AND A TIE-DYED COTTON ON THE REVERSE SIDE; MARGARET PATTERSON, MILLINER. *RIGHT:* CLOCHE WITH AN OVERSIZED, FOUR-SECTION, SHIRRED CROWN MADE FROM A BRUSHED PRINTED KNIT WITH A BLACK BOTTOM FACING; ABBY DASHER, MILLINER.

CLOCHES

LEFT: CLOCHE MADE FROM A GREEN TWEED AND TRIMMED WITH APPLIQUÉS AND A WORKING ZIPPER; A REMOVABLE CROWN OR BRIM MAY BE WORN INDIVIDUALLY; SUNG LIM LEE, MILLINER. ***RIGHT:*** CLOCHE WITH AN UPTURNED BRIM AND A PILLBOX-STYLE CROWN MADE OF STRAW CLOTH; OSNAT LUSTIG, MILLINER.

SHIRRED BERETS

LEFT: A PLEATED BERET MADE FROM A PRINTED COTTON BANDANNA; ARTHUR BANNER, MILLINER.
RIGHT: A SHIRRED BERET MADE FROM A BLACK VELVET AND TRIMMED WITH A SATIN BOW; ANNA KIM, MILLINER.

MULTI-SECTION BERETS

LEFT: AN EIGHT-SECTION BERET MADE FROM A NATURAL BURLAP AND EMBROIDERED BLACK FABRIC AND TRIMMED WITH BLACK RIKRAK AND A GOLD METAL BUTTON; KIMBERLY D'AURAIA, MILLINER.
RIGHT: A SIX-SECTION BERET MADE FROM AN EMBOSSED BLACK VINYL AND TRIMMED WITH A SILVER CHAIN; ELSIE YOFFI, MILLINER

VISORS

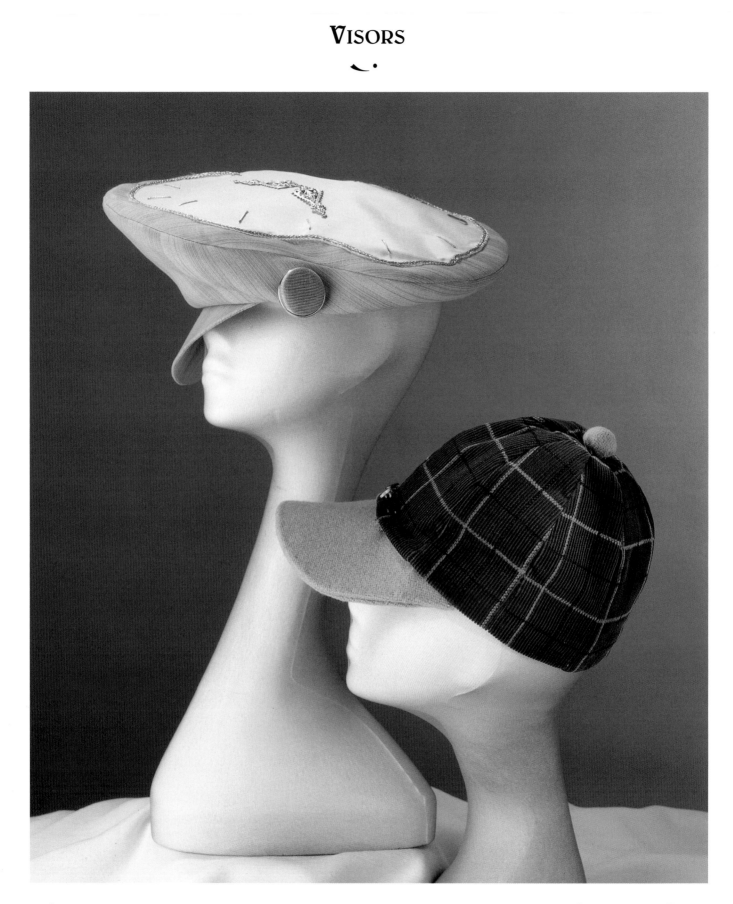

LEFT: AN ASYMMETRICAL STYLIZED BERET WITH A VISOR, INSPIRED BY THE MELTING CLOCKS THEME OF SPANISH ARTIST SALVADOR DALI; MADE FROM A BEIGE AND WHITE COTTON AND TRIMMED WITH GOLD ROPE, METAL CLOCK HANDS, AND A SIDE BUTTON; CAROL BYRD-BREDBENNER, MILLINER. *RIGHT:* A BASEBALL-CAP STYLE HAT WITH A REMOVABLE VISOR AND BUTTON TRIM; THE FOUR-SECTION CROWN IS MADE FROM A GREEN PLAID CORDUROY AND THE VISOR IS MADE FROM A YELLOW WOVEN WOOL; SUNG LIM LEE, MILLINER.

BOATERS

LEFT: A BOATER MADE FROM A SEWN WIDE BLACK STRAW BRAID AND TRIMMED WITH RED RIBBON ROSETTES, BLACK/RED VEILING, AND COQ FEATHERS; KIMBERLY D'AURAIA, MILLINER. *RIGHT:* A BOATER COVERED WITH A SHIRRED, MULTI-STRIPE JACQUARD IN BLACK/RED/BLUE/WHITE AND TRIMMED WITH A BLACK, FULL-FACE VEIL, BLACK RIBBON, AND BLACK RIBBON STANDING LOOPS; OSNAT LUSTIG, MILLINER.

BOATER

An oversized Boater covered with printed upholstery cotton and trimmed with a pale blue organza strip; Osnat Lustig, milliner.

STYLIZED BRIM

AN UPTURNED STYLIZED BRIM COVERED WITH ULTRASUEDE IN A BROWN AND ANIMAL PRINT AND
LACED UP WITH A BLACK CORD TIED TO A BOW; CAROL BYRD-BREDBENNER, MILLINER.

STYLIZED BRIM

A PROFILE HAT WITH A STYLIZED BRIM COVERED IN SILVER AND BLACK BROCADE AND TRIMMED WITH LACE RIBBON; JEAN SMITH, MILLINER.

STYLIZED BRIM

A PROFILE HAT WITH AN UPTURNED, STYLIZED BRIM COVERED WITH PURPLE AND BLACK LACE AND A CROWN COVERED WITH PURPLE VELVET; SANDRA WALCOTT TABB, MILLINER.

STYLIZED BRIM

A MUSHROOM-STYLIZED BRIM WITH THE CROWN AND TOP FACING COVERED WITH A NATURAL LINEN AND A BOTTOM FACING IN PRINTED RAYON, TRIMMED WITH A STARCHED, PLEATED BOW; OSNAT LUSTIG, MILLINER.

GARLANDS

LEFT: GARLAND MADE WITH YELLOW ROSES AND GREEN LEAVES WITH RIBBON STREAMERS AND TULLE TRAIN; DANIELLE FONTAINE, MILLINER. **CENTER:** GARLAND MADE OF VARIETY OF FLOWERS AND WAXED LEAVES WITH VELVET RIBBON STREAMERS; PAULA BRUNO, MILLINER. **RIGHT:** GARLAND MADE OF LARGE PINK ROSES AND GREEN LEAVES WITH A PINK AND WHITE TULLE TRAIN; DANIELLE FONTAINE, MILLINER.

COCKTAIL CAP

A TEARDROP SHAPED COCKTAIL CAP COVERED WITH HAND-GATHERED BROWN VELVET AND TRIMMED WITH PEARLS, A HORSE-HAIR BOW, HACKLE FEATHERS, AND A FULL-FACE VEIL; MYRA GOLDICK, MILLINER.

COCKTAIL CAPS

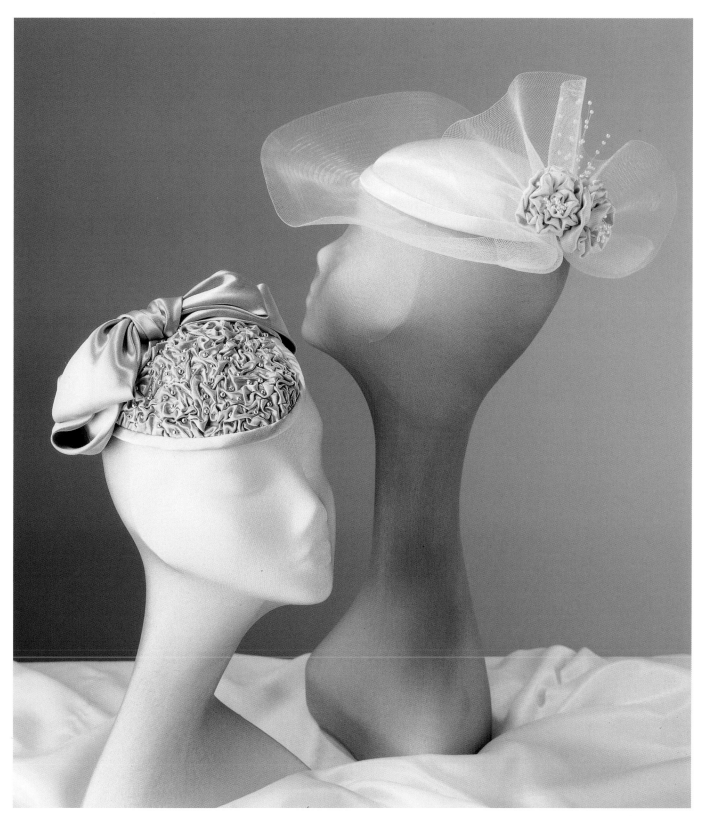

LEFT: A JULIET-SHAPED COCKTAIL CAP COVERED WITH HAND-GATHERED SILVER SATIN AND TRIMMED WITH A SELF-FABRIC DOUBLE BOW; DANIELLE FONTAINE, MILLINER. *RIGHT:* A JULIET-SHAPED COCK-TAIL CAP COVERED WITH WHITE BRIDAL SATIN WITH A WHITE HORSE-HAIR BRIM AND TRIMMED WITH SELF-FABRIC ROSETTES, A PEARL SPRAY, AND A HORSE HAIR BOW; DANIELLE FONTAINE, MILLINER.

COCKTAIL CAP

A JULIET-SHAPED COCKTAIL CAP COVERED WITH WHITE LINEN AND TRIMMED WITH SHIRRED PINK HORSE HAIR AND FLOWERS MADE FROM WHITE STOCKINGS AND WIRE; KIMBERLY D'AURAIA, MILLINER.

COCKTAIL CAP

A JULIET-SHAPED COCKTAIL CAP COVERED WITH PRINTED BROCADE AND TRIMMED WITH GREEN RIB-
BON, A HORSEHAIR BOW, AND A BOW MADE FROM GREEN VEILING; LINDA DIAN POLICHETTI,
MILLINER.

33

FEATHER PAD HATS

LEFT: A SIMPLE FELT CROWN COVERED WITH RED DYED HACKLE PADS AND TRIMMED WITH A RED MARABOU POMPON AND STRIPPED COQ FEATHERS; ANN ALBRIZIO, MILLINER. **CENTER:** A BRIMMED FELT HAT COVERED WITH BLACK DYED HACKLE PADS AND TRIMMED WITH A BLACK OSTRICH PLUME; ANN ALBRIZIO, MILLINER. **RIGHT:** A SIMPLE FELT CROWN COVERED WITH DYED HACKLE PADS IN FUCHSIA AND BLACK; SANDRA D. MANIGAULT, MILLINER.

FEATHER PAD HATS

LEFT: A FELT BERET COVERED WITH DYED PURPLE HACKLE PADS AND TRIMMED WITH PURPLE FEATHERS; ANN ALBRIZIO, MILLINER. RIGHT: A BRIMMED FELT HAT COVERED WITH TURQUOISE HACKLE PADS WITH A DYED OSTRICH PLUME POMPON; ANN ALBRIZIO, MILLINER.

ONE-BY-ONE FEATHER HATS

LEFT: A BRIMMED FELT HAT COVERED WITH INDIVIDUAL RAW RING-NECK PHEASANT FEATHERS AFFIXED TO THE HAT IN THE SAME ORDER THEY APPEAR ON THE BIRD ITSELF; ANN ALBRIZIO, MILLINER. *RIGHT:* A BRIMMED FELT HAT COVERED WITH INDIVIDUAL DYED TURKEY FLATS FEATHERS ON THE BRIM AND TIP; THE SIDE BAND IS COVERED WITH INDIVIDUAL RAW PHEASANT FEATHERS; ANN ALBRIZIO, MILLINER.

ONE-BY-ONE FEATHER HATS

LEFT: A SIMPLE FELT CROWN COVERED WITH INDIVIDUAL DYED COQ FEATHERS AND TRIMMED WITH RHINE-STONES; ANN ALBRIZIO, MILLINER. *RIGHT:* A BRIMMED FELT HAT COVERED WITH INDIVIDUAL DEGRADED (BLEACHED) TURKEY FLATS FEATHERS (TIP AND BRIM) AND RAW PHEASANT FEATHERS (SIDE BAND), AND TRIMMED WITH RAW HACKLE FEATHERS AND RHINESTONES; ANN ALBRIZIO, MILLINER.

FEATHERS

TOP ROW: ACID BURNT OSTRICH PLUME. **SECOND ROW:** STRUNG DYED COQ FEATHERS (BLACK), PHEASANT TAIL FEATHERS (LONG AND SHORT). **THIRD ROW:** STRUNG RAW SCHLAPPEN, STRUNG DYED GOOSE NAGOIRES, STRUNG RAW SCHLAPPEN. **FOURTH ROW:** PADS (GUINEA HEN DYED YELLOW, PHEASANT DYED RED, RAW PHEASANT), STRUNG BLEACHED NECK HACKLE, STRUNG BURNT PEACOCK HERL, STRUNG RAW PEACOCK HERL. **FIFTH ROW:** STRUNG RAW GOOSE COQUILLE, INDIVIDUAL HACKLE, STRUNG HACKLE. **SIXTH ROW:** DYED TURKEY PLUMAGE, DYED TURKEY FLAT, DYED MARABOU. **SEVENTH ROW:** BIOTS, QUILL, DYED OSTRICH PLUME (SHORT, MEDIUM AND LONG).

FEATHER TRIMS

COUNTER CLOCKWISE STARTING FROM LEFT: COQ-TAIL COCKTAIL, BOA POMPON (DYED TURKEY PLUMAGE), PLUMAGE ROSE WITH COQ FEATHERS CENTER, PLUMAGE ROSE WITH STRIPPED COQ FEATHERS AND BURNT PEACOCK HERLS CENTER, CURLED TAIL FEATHER (BURNT OSTRICH PLUME).

GETTING STARTED

M AKING CUSTOM HATS IS INTIMATE AND PERSONAL WORK. MILLINERY IS LEARNED BY DOING. THE MORE HATS YOU MAKE, THE MORE FAMILIAR YOU WILL BE WITH THE PROPERTIES OF DIFFERENT FABRICS, FOUNDATION MATERIALS, AND TRIMS—AND THE MORE SKILLFUL YOU WILL BECOME IN USING THE TOOLS OF THE TRADE.

ALL OF THE INFORMATION IN THIS SECTION WILL CONTRIBUTE TO YOUR SUCCESS AS A MILLINER. THESE ARE THE BASICS, AND YOU SHOULD NOT START WITHOUT THEM. FILL YOUR MILLINERY TOOLBOX WITH THIS KNOWLEDGE AND YOU WILL ENJOY MAKING GREAT HATS.

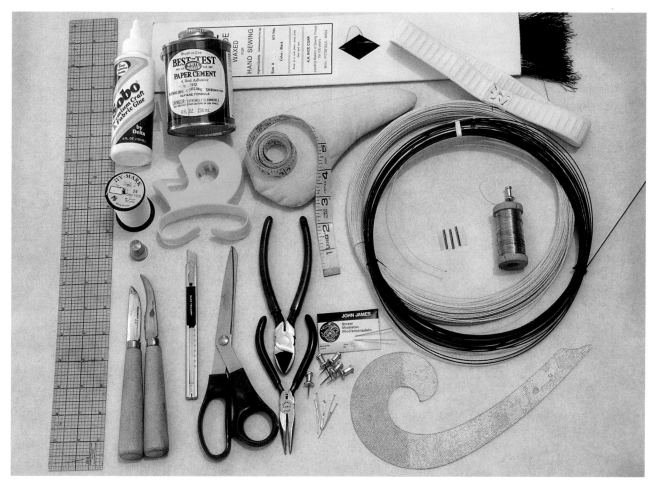

Assorted tools and materials

MATERIALS AND EQUIPMENT

FOUNDATION MATERIALS

Buckram ⌐ A woven material covered with water-based sizing, buckram is pliable when wet and can be shaped over a hat block. It is available in two colors, black and white. Millinery grade #625 buckram is used as a foundation fabric for making hat frames. (See Figure 1.)

Flexie (Flexible buckram) ⌐ Flexie is a loosely woven, flexible foundation material. Very lightly sized, it is lighter

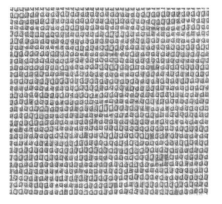

Figure 1

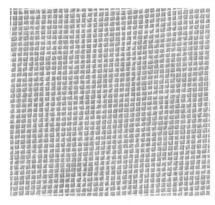

Figure 2

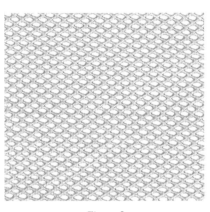

Figure 3

Figure 4

Figure 5

in weight and softer, and is usually used on the bias. (See Figure 2.)

Cape Net ~ Cape net is a lightweight, open-mesh material covered with a heavy, water-based sizing. It is used for blocking soft frames (as for cocktail caps). The material is visually pleasing, so no lining is needed. (See Figure 3.)

French Net ~ This lighter version of cape net is, unfortunately, no longer available commercially in many places.

French Elastic ~ This unsized, closely woven fabric is lighter in weight than the flexie, and is used when light but firm support is needed. (See Figure 4.)

French Elastic Bias Tape ~ Used as a seam binding, the close weave of French elastic bias tape conceals the edge wires and raw edges of hat frames. The tape can be purchased precut to a 1-inch-wide (2.5 cm) bias strip in large rolls. If you do not have one readily available, use one of the many commercial bias tapes sold in sewing-supply stores in several widths and in many colors. Before using, spread out the folded edges and iron them flat to prevent bulkiness.

Flalean ~ Flalean is a stable cotton fabric with a brushed flannel pile on one side and a smooth surface on the other side. It is used as an interlining with the smooth side facing out. (See Figure 5.)

Muslin ~ Heavyweight grades of muslin are used as interlining and pressing cloths.

Lining ~ Bridal satin and taffeta have the substantial feel required of millinery lining material and are available in many colors.

WIRE

Frame Wire ~ Frame wire is the most common wire used in millinery, both for reinforcing brim and crown edges and for foundation work. It is covered with paper or rayon and is available in black and white. The most useful sizes to purchase are #19 and #21. Frame wire is generally sold in large coils of about 60 yards (54 m), but suppliers will often sell smaller rolls or short ends as well.

Steel Wire ~ Number 19 uncovered steel wire is used for brims that must lie perfectly flat, such as a sailor brim. Steel wire is hard and springy, so always wear safety goggles when handling it.

Wire Joiners ~ Wire joiners are small, hollow metal tubes of varying lengths and diameters used to secure the ends of the steel wire. To use them, insert the ends of the steel wire into the open ends of the tubes as deep as they can go, then crimp the tube flat with needle nose pliers.

Tie Wire – Fine tie wire, #34, is used for joining the cross sections of a wire frame, for tying loops of ribbon bows together, and for bunching flowers for trimming.

IMPLEMENTS

Steamer – A steady, regulated source of steam is essential for millinery work. Most industrial shops and workrooms are equipped with commercial boilers and steam tables for steaming felt and straw. Portable steamers provide a less elaborate alternative, but be sure to purchase a quality brand. (I use the Jiffy J-1 model.)

Irons – Plain and steam irons are available in professional and home models. Professional irons commonly have an external water reservoir, allowing for longer periods between refilling it and a continuous flow of steam when needed. Home models have built-in water reservoirs and offer various levels of steam bursts. Choose one that suits your needs and budget. With either type of iron, the surface must be kept smooth and clean since dirt and stains easily transfer to fabrics. If a nonsteam setting is used, you may need a damp cloth for steam pressing.

Portable millinery steamer

Pressing Roll – This clever, easy-to-make accessory is used for ironing curved areas that cannot be pressed flat. Appendix III provides instructions for making one.

Spray Sizing – Available in aerosol form, spray sizing is used to add light stiffness to fabrics, silk flowers, and ribbons.

Hat Stretcher – This mechanical device has a built-in heating element and is useful for pressing the inside of a hat for a professional look, as well as for increasing hat size up to an inch. Simply dampen a ribbon with a wet sponge and place over the hot block for a few minutes.

Electric hat stretcher

Sewing Machine – Professional millinery sewing machines are difficult to find and quite expensive. There are several types and each one is designed to perform a special task. A home sewing machine equipped with a freearm will work fine for most basic sewing functions. Set the stitch length to eight stitches per inch as in the professional machines.

Measuring Tools – Several kinds of measuring tools are used in the millinery shop, including a dressmaker's measuring tape for taking head size measurements, a millinery ruler made from a transparent ruler (see Appendix I for instructions), and a #17 French curve for making pattern curves.

Millinery Needles ～ Millinery needles, also known as "sharps," are longer than ordinary sewing needles. They are numbered in sequence, 3 through 10, with thicker needles having the lower numbers. For general millinery work, choose numbers 5, 6, and 7.

Millinery Threads ～ Millinery thread spools are categorized by number: the higher the number, the finer the thread. The most commonly used sizes are #24 for basting, trimming, and attaching wire to frames, and #50 for finishing work. Basting thread is used in basic colors such as black, white, gray, and brown. Finishing threads generally match the fabric's color. The basting thread is strong and slightly glazed with wax, making it easy to draw through a number of layers of material without snags.

Rice's Silamide Thread ～ This waxed thread is used for fine hand sewing. It is sold in bundle form in basic colors such as white, brown, and black, and can be obtained from millinery- and fur-supply sources.

Thimble ～ A closed metal thimble large enough to fit your third finger is essential. Pushing a needle through several layers of fabric—which is what you often have to do when making a hat—is not a job for the naked finger. Find one that fits and learn to like and use it.

Pliers ～ Two kinds of pliers are needed for millinery work: needle nose pliers for twisting wire and crimping joiners and a pair of wire-cutters for cutting wire to the proper length.

Scissors ～ A pair of good, quality dressmaker's scissors is the milliner's most important tool. They should be at least 5 inches (12.5 cm) long. Use a less expensive pair to cut paper and foundation fabrics such as buckram and flexie.

Balsa Head Block ～ Balsa blocks in the shape of human heads can be made to fit any specified headsize. (Do not confuse them with the inexpensive foam or plastic wig blocks which are often used as hat displays.) If you make hats for people other than yourself, you will need headsize blocks in several sizes—typically 22, 22½, and 23 inches (56, 57, and 59 cm)—but also in other sizes if needed.

Headsize plate (left) and balsa head block

Headsize Plate ~ This is an oval plate made from wood or cardboard cut in your headsize. It is used to mark the open end of a beret and other pattern hats. Appendix II offers a handy reference table.

Pins ~ Two kinds of pins are routinely used: dressmaker straight pins for pinning a pattern to fabric and long, metal-head pushpins, for securing the hat parts to the balsa block.

Markers ~ A tracing wheel, a pencil, and dressmaker's chalk.

Pattern Paper ~ Sold in roll form, these plain or gridded pattern papers are available in most sewing supply stores.

ADHESIVES

Fabric Adhesives ~ These water-based, white adhesives are made specifically for gluing fabrics and for attaching nonwashable trims. Read the labels carefully before using and don't be tempted to use school glues. (I like to use Sobo.)

Trim Adhesives ~ Rubber cement, a brush-on, waterproof, quick-drying adhesive, is used for gluing feathers, flowers, and ribbons.

Fusible Adhesives ~ When pressed with an iron, fusible adhesives hold trimmings such as double-sided bows or appliqués together.

NOTIONS

Some notions will be needed for every hat you make, so keep them together in a handy kit.

Scissors	**Tracing wheel**
Sharp pencil	**Pattern carbon paper**
Eraser	**Pattern paper**
Tailor's chalk	**Adhesive tape**
Dressmaker's pins	**Millinery needles**—#5, #6, #7 (or "sharps" in same sizes)
Push pins	**Basting thread**—#24
Millinery ruler	**Sewing thread**—3-ply in assorted colors (or #50 and #60 for millinery sewing machines)
#17 French curve	
Dressmaker's measuring tape	

Figure 6

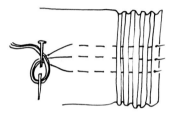

Figure 7

Figure 8

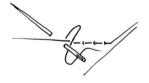

Figure 9

Figure 10

Figure 11

BASIC STITCHES

Professional-looking hats require neat, even stitches and impeccable workmanship. They can be achieved only by continuous practice and application.

Running Stitch ⌣ This is the simplest sewing stitch and is used where a strong stitch is unnecessary; when gathering, shirring, or tucking, for example. Simply pass the needle through the material, taking several small stitches at a time, then draw the needle through. (See Figure 6.)

Basting Stitch ⌣ This stitch is used to temporarily hold fabrics together, and consists of alternately long and short running stitches. When removing the basting stitches, clip the thread in a long stitch in several places, then pull threads out. (See Figure 7.)

Shirring Stitch ⌣ The shirring stitch uses even running stitches on both the wrong and right sides of fabric. Continue throughout the desired length, then draw thread together to form even gathers. (See Figure 8.)

Pick Stitch ⌣ This tiny, even stitch is done in ¼ inch (6 mm) increments and is used on some brim edges and round crowns. (See Figure 9.)

Backstitch ⌣ Use this stitch to sew two pieces of material together where strength is required. Insert the needle at the end of the last stitch and bring out the length of a stitch farther on. (See Figure 10.)

Overcast Stitch ⌣ This stitch is used to sew down the edges of material and to apply wire around the edges of brims and the welt of felt brims. Sew with close, straight stitches, bringing the needle over and over toward you. Do not take the stitches too deep or draw the thread too tight. (See Figure 11.)

Buttonhole Stitch ⌣ This stitch is used to sew wire onto frames. Take several overcasting stitches, then bring the needle down to the right depth from the wrong side. Keep the thread behind the eye and under the needle's point. (See Figure 12.)

Tie Stitch ⌣ Use this stitch to fasten trimmings and veiling on a hat. Slip the needle through the material and bring needle back through. Knot the ends and clip the thread close to the knot. (See Figure 13.)

Cross-Stitch ⌣ The cross-stitch is used to hold down labels. Work from left to right, crossing thread at each stitch. (See Figure 14.)

Slip Stitch ⌣ This stitch is used when an almost invisible stitch is needed. Work from right to left, inserting the needle through the top layer of the fabric, then catch several threads off the bottom layer (directly underneath the top one). Slip the needle between the layers, about ¼ inch to the left, and come out through the top layer again. (See Figure 15.)

Whipstitch - Use this stitch for neat edge-shirring as in French lining or the bias rosette. (See Figure 16.)

Figure 12

CHOOSING AND HANDLING FABRIC —

Not unlike a house or a car, a hat's good looks and fit rely on solid foundation, correct choice of materials, and proper construction method. It all begins with the choice of fashion fabric and hat style. In soft hats, the fabric and interlining are always used as a single unit. Some fashion fabrics have enough body of their own and need no interlining (e.g. cotton, jersey, tweed, tapestry, velveteen), and a lining material such as bridal satin or taffeta would be sufficient.

Figure 13

When the fashion fabric is fine and limp (e.g. organza, silk velvet, crepe de Chine), a foundation or interlining fabric is needed. The following fabrics make good choices.

Flexible buckram (**Flexie**), (stiff) available in either black or white.

Flalean (soft)

Hymo, lightweight, medium, or heavy, as used in tailoring.

Muslin (various weights). It can be stiffened with spray starch or by soaking the fabric in a gelatin solution, drying, and ironing it before use.

French elastic

For stiff frame construction (i.e., hat frames covered with fabric), the following materials will make a solid foundation.

Figure 14

Stiff buckram, available in either black or white

Flexible buckram (**Flexie**), available in either black or white

For foundation of bridal wear and sheer fabrics decorated with lace, beads, flowers, use:

Cape net

Lace stiffened with sizing

The lining gives a hat a neat finished look by hiding details (such as raw fabric edges) and the fashion fabric's wrong side. The lining's color may match or contrast the fashion fabric, according to the design. The weight of the material must be neither heavier nor stiffer than the fashion fabric and should be in harmony with the rest of the hat. Taffeta, bridal satin, and crepe de Chine make good lining materials.

Figure 15

Figure 16

Figure 17

Figure 18

Figure 19

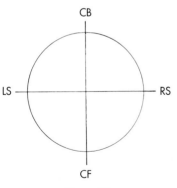

Figure 20

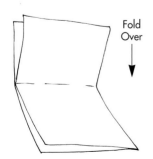

Figure 21

The following fabrics require special handling.

Velvet ⌐ Never iron velvet or you will crush the pile and lose the 'velvet' look. Instead, gently steam it to remove any wrinkles. When storing velvet, try to roll or hang it because a fold can form a permanent crushed velvet crease.

Satin ⌐ It is best to steam wrinkles out of satin as well, because hot irons can discolor the fabric and water will most likely stain it.

Sheer and Fine Fabrics ⌐ Fabrics such as crepe de Chine, organza, and chiffon need to be carefully sewn with sharp, new needles. A dull needle can cause puckering of the fabric. Here, too, steam wrinkles out rather than using an iron.

When in doubt use common sense and practice on scraps of fabric before risking your investment.

MEASURING THE HEAD

The first step to a perfect fit is recognizing that the shape of human the head is an oval! In general, human heads are longer front to back and narrower side to side. Prove it to yourself by placing a round saucepan on your head as if it were a hat. Notice how much room is left on the sides, right above the ears. When this "extra" is removed, you're left with an oval shape.

Next, as in garments, heads come in all sizes. Some are small and some are large. When you measure the head, be sure to consider not only the hat style but also the amount of hair and hairstyle. A hat's fit should be light and comfortable, not burdensome.

Measure the headsize horizontally above the eyebrows, around the largest part of the head. Do not wrap the measuring tape around the head too tightly or the hat will not have a comfortable fit. Leave a "pinkie's" worth of ease. Write down the size in inches or centimeters. Adult women's sizes average 22½ to 23 inches (57 to 58.5 cm) with a slight trend in recent years toward larger head sizes.

For fitted hats, such as turban and cloche, additional measurements are needed.

⌐ Around the head (See Figure 17.)

⌐ Center front to center back (See Figure 18.)

⌐ Side to side, including the ears if style requires (See Figure 19.)

Before you begin to work on a design, transfer the appropriate marking to the head block. If you plan to make more than one hat for the same person, consider preparing a personal information card with favorite colors, materials, styles, and measurements.

USEFUL PRACTICES

KEY TO ABBREVIATIONS

The following abbreviations are used in text and figures throughout this book. (See Figure 20.)

CF - Center Front

CB - Center Back

LS - Left Side

RS - Right Side

FINDING THE CENTER OF A SHEET OF PATTERN PAPER WITHOUT MEASURING

Fold the sheet in half and then in half again. Unfold the paper. The point where the vertical and horizontal creases meet is the center of the sheet. Draw pencil lines along the creases. (See Figures 21 and 22.)

TRUE BIAS

All woven fabrics consist of strong fibers that go lengthwise (also called warp) and lead the main grain direction. The fibers that are woven into the warp crosswise (also called weft) fill the gap. Neither grain direction provides much stretch and drape.

In millinery, both stretch and drape are very important, and to attain them in fabric, only true bias is used. True bias is the line measured 45° to the weft or the warp. To find a true bias on any fabric, follow Figure 23.

TRUING A DRAFT

Whenever a draft is designed by using the slash and shape method (stylized beret, stylized brim, or cloche), it is necessary to make the outline of the flat draft even and uninterrupted. The accepted method is called *truing* and is done by using the #17 French curve. Place the French curve along the draft outline while trying to find a section on it that will match the curve. Then run a pencil point along the curve, smoothing out any irregularities. (See Figure 24.)

ANATOMY OF A HAT

Beret ～ tip, facing, band (See Figure 25.)

Pillbox ～ tip, side band (See Figure 26.)

Brimmed Hat ～ crown, collar, brim (See Figure 27.)

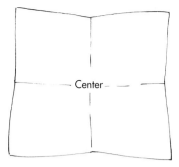

Center

Figure 22

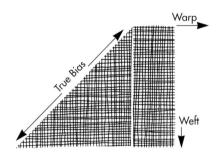

Warp

True Bias

Weft

Figure 23

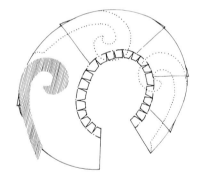

Figure 24

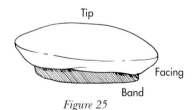

Tip

Facing

Band

Figure 25

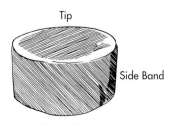

Tip

Side Band

Figure 26

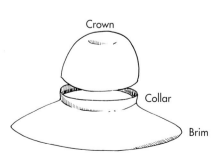

Crown

Collar

Brim

Figure 27

PROPORTION AND BALANCE IN HAT STYLES

The style of a hat is determined by shape, color, and texture. Although hats can vary in style, there are two major factors that make a hat flattering and beautiful on the wearer—proportion and balance.

Proportion is the visual relationship between the crown, brim, and trimming. A balanced hat will not have one side outweigh the other, whether it is a symmetrical hat (e.g., boater, turban) or an asymmetrical one (e.g., profile brim, beret).

You can turn a dull, ill-proportioned hat, such as one with a brim width that equals the crown height, into a more exciting creation by simply adding color and trim. For example, if you made the hat that is described above in a light-colored crown and a dark-colored brim, you would notice that the crown appears larger than the brim.

Generally, when designing a hat, the crown should not be narrower or wider than the head.

Often hats look best when they have a single focal point. So if the brim is small or there's no brim at all (pill box), the focal point is the crown. It could have an unusual trim, or size (extra tall), or whimsical shape, or special color.

Conversely, if the brim is the prominent feature, then the crown needs to be subtle. If the trim is the most important part of the hat, then make it extra special by keeping the brim and crown in the background. Use quiet colors, minimize surface texture, or even make the brim and crown smaller.

Sensing balance can come only with practice. Train your eye to identify and judge what looks becoming on the wearer. For example, an asymmetrical design would be suitable for most face types but particularly good for full and round ones. Sometimes, a simple change in the position of the trim or placement of the hat on the head may result in a marked improvement of proportion and balance or both.

MILLINERY RIBBONS

Of all the wonderful ribbons out there, everything except millinery ribbon is suitable only for trimming. In the following examples you will see why the millinery ribbon is so unique. One sign of a quality hat is a well-fitting sweatband. The sweatband lines the hat where it touches the forehead, thus protecting the hat itself from makeup and perspiration stains. When the sweatband begins to look worn and dirty, you should replace it with a fresh one. Sweatbands can also add a decorative accent to a hat by using a contrasting colored ribbon. In a later chapter you will learn how to use the millinery ribbon as a trim by itself and in an assortment of decorative bows.

Millinery ribbon is often confused with grosgrain ribbon. On the surface they look alike, but a closer inspection easily reveals the differences.

Grosgrain ribbon is a closely woven, ribbed ribbon with defined crosswise thread and a smooth edge. Grosgrain is generally made of polyester, giving it a crisp, stable feel, and is available in many colors and patterns. These ribbons are most suitable for trimming. (See Figure 28.)

Millinery (belting) ribbon is very similar in appearance to grosgrain ribbon, but there are two important elements that tell them apart. First, millinery ribbon has a saw tooth edge. Second, millinery ribbon is made of at least 50% cotton blended with rayon or silk, giving it a supple, flexible feel. Millinery ribbon can be swirled and manipulated into shape with a steam iron. This special ribbon is available from millinery supply sources in solid colors and in several widths. (See Figure 29.)

The following conversion table shows today's standard ribbon codes and equivalent widths. Unlisted widths are no longer commercially made, although you might be able to find limited quantities in antique stores.

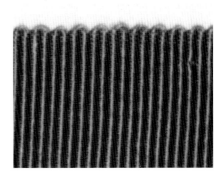

Figure 28

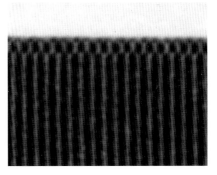

Figure 29

Number	Width in Inches	Width in Millimeters
1	¼	6.5
2	½	13
3	⅝	16
5	⅞	23
9	1½	38
12	1¾	45
16	2⅛	54
40	3	76
100	4³⁄₁₆	107

SWIRLING A RIBBON

Swirling is done so the ribbon will fit the crown properly. Most crowns are shaped or tapered, not straight cylinders. Swirling allows the ribbon to conform to the crown's true shape. For cylindrical crowns, such as in pillbox and boater styles, swirling the ribbon is not necessary.

First, measure and cut the needed length of millinery ribbon. Place the ribbon on an ironing board with a steam iron on top of the ribbon's right end. Weigh the ribbon down so it won't move. Grip the ribbon with your other hand and pull it slightly toward the left side and downward, in an arched motion. (See Figure 30.) At the same time, let the iron travel along the ribbon following the same curved path. The result: a curved ribbon. Try it out on the hat and reswirl if necessary.

Figure 30

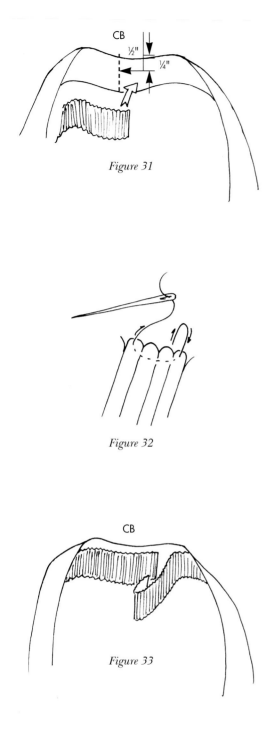

Figure 31

Figure 32

Figure 33

INSERTING A SWEATBAND RIBBON ——

⌣ Measure a millinery ribbon length equal to the headsize and add 1 inch (2.5 cm).

⌣ Swirl the ribbon if the hat style calls for it.

⌣ Measure ½ inch (13 mm) to the right of the center back mark, and place the cut edge of the ribbon there. (See Figure 31.)

⌣ Lower the ribbon to ¼ inch (6.5 mm) below the edge of the headsize so the sweatband ribbon will remain invisible.

⌣ Using a millinery needle #5 and a strong thread color-matched to the ribbon, secure the ribbon end to the hat with a ¼-inch pick stitch. The needle travels ¼ inch under the ribbon and emerges through one of the loops along its edge, then goes under for another ¼ inch, and so on. (See Figure 32.)

⌣ When you return to the center back mark, there should be an extra ½-inch length of ribbon left. Fold it under itself so the fold lines up with the center back mark and the cut edges line up as well. (See Figure 33.)

⌣ Secure the ribbon through all layers.

⌣ *Helpful Hint* ⌣

Before you start sewing the ribbon, pin it all around to the headsize. Pinning will verify that the correct side of the swirl is aligned with the headsize and that the ribbon does not shift while you are stitching.

FINISHING TOUCHES ——————

Traditionally, custom-made hats have center front marked on the sweatband with a small embroidered asterisk (∗) or plus (+) signs in a contrasting color. If you have a label, sew it over and across the center back using a strong stitch such as the cross-stitch. (You want it to stay permanently on the hat as a reminder to the wearer that you are ready to make many more beautiful hats for her.)

Always remember to swirl the ribbon where appropriate! The hat will look better and will have a custom-made quality.

SOFT HATS

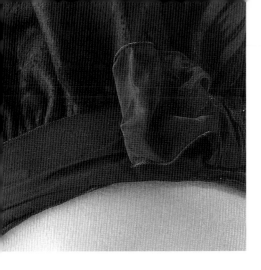

THE SHIRRED BERET

T HE BERET HAS RETAINED ITS BASIC SHAPE FOR MORE THAN 2,500 YEARS BECAUSE IT IS BOTH SIMPLE AND VERSATILE—A HAT THAT CAN BE WORN IN A MONARCH'S PALACE OR IN AN ARTIST'S STUDIO. BERETS CAN BE MADE FROM ALMOST ANY MATERIAL, FROM SIMPLE WOOL FELT TO THE MOST LUXURIOUS SILK OR VELVET. THEY CAN BE DECORATED WITH THE MOST FANCIFUL TRIMMINGS OR WITH NOTHING AT ALL. THE BERET IS, CLEARLY, A HAT FOR ALL SEASONS.

MATERIALS

½ yard (.45 m) fashion fabric (wool, tweed, velvet, cotton, etc.)

½ yard lining material (bridal satin or taffeta)

#9 millinery ribbon cut to the headsize length plus 1 inch (2.5 cm)

1-inch-wide strip of stiff buckram cut on straight grain to the headsize plus 2 inches (5 cm)

color-matched #24 basting thread and #50 sewing thread

#5 and #6 millinery needles

Millinery ruler

Pattern paper

Scissors, measuring tape, pencil, straight pins, pushpins

Headsize plate and balsa block

PATTERN DEVELOPMENT

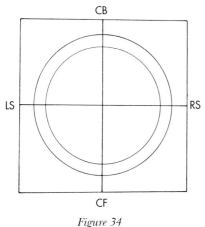

Figure 34

❧ Fold the pattern paper in half and half again. Unfold. Draw a line along the vertical fold and mark it as the straight grain line. Draw a second line along the horizontal fold. Where the lines cross each other is the center of the sheet.

❧ Using the millinery ruler, pencil, and pushpin, draw two circles on the pattern paper, the first a large circle 18 inches (46 cm) in diameter, and within it a second circle, ½ inch (13 mm) smaller. Mark the smaller circle as the seam line. Draw a line through the center of the circle to indicate center front (CF), and back (CB); a second line perpendicular to the first will indicate left and right sides (LS, RS). (See Figure 34.)

CUTTING

- Layer the fashion fabric and lining with wrong sides facing each other and pin them together as one piece. This is the only time in hat pattern work that the fashion fabric and the lining are cut as a single unit. (See Figure 35.)
- Trace pattern lines onto the fabric, and cut out through both layers.
- To make a headband, cut a 2-inch-wide (5 cm) fabric strip on a true bias with its length being the headsize plus a ½-inch seam allowance around the band. (See Figure 36.)

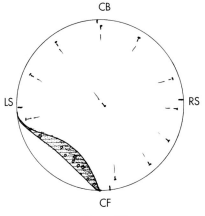

Figure 35

CONSTRUCTION

- Using #24 thread and a #5 needle, baste through all layers along the seam line all around the circle.
- Halfway between the seam line and the outer edge (¼ inch, 6.5 mm, in from the outer edge), sew an even running stitch with #24 thread in color matching the fashion fabric. Before you begin, make sure there is enough thread to go all around the circle and securely knot the end of the thread.
- Repeat the steps above ¼ inch below the seam line. There should now be three rows of stitching:
  1. A running stitch ¼ inch from the edge.
  2. A white basting stitch ½ inch from the edge (seam line).
  3. A second running stitch ¼ inch below the basting stitch. (See Figure 37.)
- Perfect shirring requires patience.
- Pull all threads (above and below the seam line) from one end, shifting and gathering the fabric along the thread. When half the circle is gathered, secure the thread ends by twisting them around a straight pin. Pull the threads from the other end to shirr the remaining half circle. (See Figure 38.) To make sure that the finished beret fits correctly, place it on the balsa headblock. Distribute the gathers evenly and tie the thread ends together.

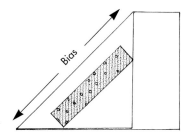

Figure 36

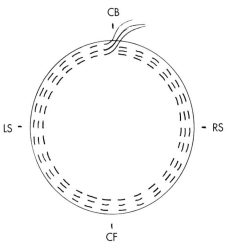

Figure 37

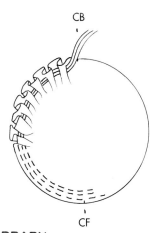

Figure 38

~·· *Helpful Hint* ~··

For an oversized beret, such as a chef's hat, the diameter of the circle could be as large as 25 inches (64 cm). A circle smaller than 12 inches (30 cm) in diameter, however, will not give you enough material to work with.

55

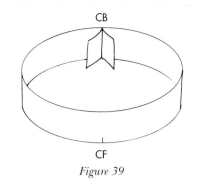

CB

CF

Figure 39

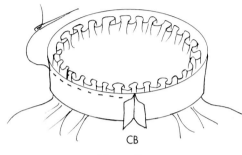

CB

Figure 40

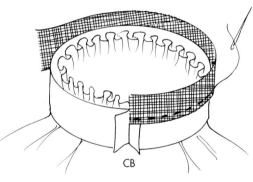

CB

Figure 41

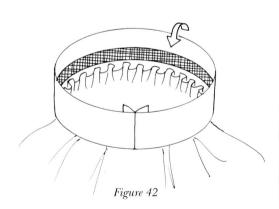

Figure 42

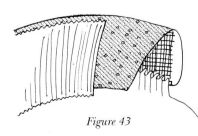

Figure 43

Headband

- Join the short ends of the band to form a circle. Press the open seam with a steam iron. Be careful not to stretch the band, since being cut on a true bias makes it dimensionally unstable. Mark the center front (CF) and center back (CB) with a contrasting color thread, noting that the joined ends will be at the center back of the hat. (See Figure 39.)

- Pin the headband's seam line to the seam line of the hat, matching CF, CB, and sides. Baste the band to the beret all around, using a small backstitch. (See Figure 40.)

- Cut a 1-inch-wide buckram strip on a straight grain the length of your head size plus 1 inch added to each end. Bend it into a loop, and overlap 1 inch on each side. Check for proper fit on the headsize block or plate, then secure the overlap with a strong stitch.

- Baste the buckram strip over the stitched shirring and the headband using a basting stitch. (See Figure 41.)

- Flip the headband over and under, covering the buckram strip. This will give the headband a smooth appearance. (See Figure 42.)

- Turn the remaining part of the headband up into the beret, "encasing" the buckram strip. (See Figure 43.) The straight grain buckram controls the bias headband and guarantees proper fit. Tuck the seam allowance under and finish off with a small stitch. If the fabric is heavy, the shirring may be rather thick. Trim off any excess thickness with scissors, giving the beret a smooth look and feel.

- Finally, sew in the sweatband using #9 millinery ribbon, referring to page 52 for the proper technique.

- Place the hat on the balsa block. Carefully steam out any wrinkles, and set aside to dry for at least ten minutes. As a finishing touch, trim the completed beret with a flower or a bow.

~· Helpful Hint ~·

You can make a shirred beret from a piece of fabric as small as half a yard! Shop for remnants of unusual fabrics to make a special hat. Choose fabric with 'feel,' such as tapestry or wool, but stay away from taffeta! Taffeta is most suitable for lining use.

Use the same pattern to make a draw string or snap-top purse; or, make a matching scarf using the hat fabric or complementary solid color.

THE TWO-SECTION BERET

T HE TWO-SECTION BERET IS ANOTHER BASIC HAT PATTERN. LIKE THE SHIRRED BERET, IT IS VERSATILE AND CAN BE BOTH CASUAL AND TAILORED.

MATERIALS

½ yard (.45 m) fashion fabric

½ yard lining material (bridal satin or taffeta)

½ yard interlining material (if fashion fabric is lightweight)

#9 millinery ribbon cut to the headsize plus 1 inch (2.5 cm)

1-inch-wide buckram strip, cut on the straight grain to a length of the headsize plus 2 inches (5 cm)

color-matched #24 basting thread and #50 sewing thread

#5 and #6 millinery needles

Millinery ruler

Two sheets pattern paper, both 20-inch (50 cm) squares

Scissors, measuring tape, pencil, long metal-head pushpins, straight pins

Headsize plate and balsa headblock

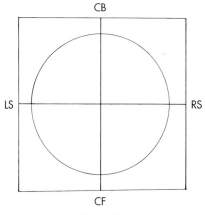

Figure 44

PATTERN DEVELOPMENT

❧ Fold the pattern paper in half and in half again. Draw a line along the vertical fold and mark it as the straight grain line. Draw a second line along the horizontal fold. Where the lines cross each other is the center of the sheet.

❧ Using a millinery ruler, draw a 10- to 15-inch-diameter (25 - 38 cm) circle on each sheet. Mark CF, CB, LS, RS on each circle. NOTE: One circle will be the pattern for the tip of the beret and the other will be its facing. Mark them accordingly. (See Figure 44.)

❧ Place the headsize plate on the center of the facing circle only, then slide it toward the center back so it is off the center line by about 2 inches. Trace this line to the pattern paper. It is the seam line. (See Figure 45.) Caution: If you leave less than 2 inches from the back (measuring from the headsize line to the edge of the beret) the hat will not fit well.

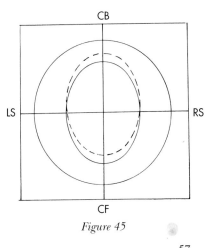

Figure 45

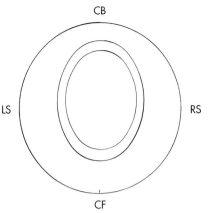

Figure 46

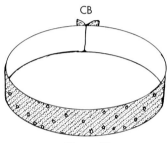

Figure 47

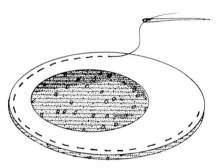

Figure 48

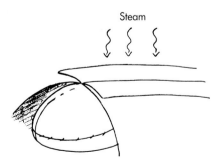

Figure 49

Before cutting out the pattern add a ½-inch (13 mm) seam allowance all around the outer edge. The headsize on the "facing" pattern is tricky! Seam allowance there really means that it must be ½ inch smaller than the actual headsize plate. (See Figure 46.)

- For the headband, cut a 2-inch-wide (5 cm) bias strip in head-size circumference with a ½-inch seam allowance on each side. The back seam will be straight. (See Figure 47.)

CUTTING

- Transfer the pattern markings to the fabric and cut out the facing and head band. If the selected fashion fabric is light-weight, you will need interlining. Interlining acts as a foundation and any of the following would be a good choice: Muslin, light French elastic, or Flalean. Stay stitch the interlining and outer fabric together at the edges and use them as a single piece.
- Cut the lining ¼ inch (6.5 mm) smaller than the pattern. No headband is needed for the lining.

CONSTRUCTION

Tip and Facing

- Baste or pin the tip and facing circles with right sides together, then stitch either by hand with a small backstitch or by machine. Assemble the lining in the same fashion. (See Figure 48.)
- Press the seam open for good, rounded effect, using a small pressing roll. (See Figure 49.)
- Turn the assembled lining inside out and insert the lining into the sewn beret. The lining should fit snugly inside the beret.

Headband

- There are many ways of making a headband, but once you grasp the basic concept, you can come up with design of your own. For a basic headband, all you have to do is stitch the short ends of the bias strip together, either by hand or by machine, and press the seam open.
- To make a simple headband, take a 1-inch (2.5 cm) buckram strip cut on a straight grain, bend it into a loop, and overlap 1 inch on each side. Check for proper fit on the headsize block or plate, and secure with a strong stitch. Note: The

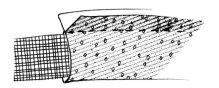

Figure 50

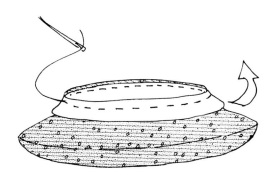

Figure 51

headband should always be cut on the bias, with straight grain reinforcement of buckram.

- Fold the fabric headband in half lengthwise. Place the buckram band along the center fold, matching center back stitch lines. The fabric band should encase the buckram and have a ½-inch seam allowance of fabric along the open edge of the band. (See Figure 50.)

- Baste the fabric band along the seam line, encasing the buckram securely inside. The straight seam on the band indicates the center back of the beret.

- Place the band on the seam line of the beret, matching CF,CB, LS, RS markings. When you have both seam lines aligned, sew them together securely using a back stitch. (See Figure 51.)

- Flip the headsize band over; the beret is almost completed.

FINISHING

Inserting the Sweatband

- Lightly swirl #9 millinery ribbon that has been carefully placed on the headband. Sew the ribbon along the edge of the connecting seams of the hat and the band to cover the ragged edge. Stitch either by hand or machine as described on page 52.

- When the beret is complete, place it on the balsa block and steam to remove any wrinkles and to set the shape. Never take the hat off immediately after steaming or it will lose its shape. Let it dry for at least ten minutes. The exact drying time will, of course, depend on the temperature and humidity of your workroom.

- Trim the completed hat with a self-fabric, making a bow or flower.

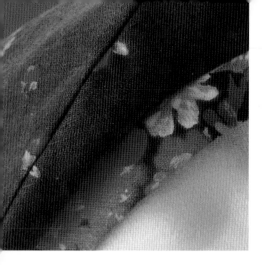

STYLIZED BERET

T HE OTHER BERETS IN THIS CHAPTER REQUIRE SOME MANIPULATION AND ARRANGING OF THE FABRIC FOLDS WHEN YOU WEAR THEM. THE STYLIZED BERET, HOWEVER, IS DESIGNED TO LOOK JUST RIGHT FROM THE MOMENT YOU PUT IT ON. THE REASON? ITS FACING (THE BOTTOM PART OF THE HAT) IS STYLED SO IT HAS NO EXCESS FULLNESS, AND IS CREATED WITH A SPECIAL SLASH AND SHAPE TECHNIQUE.

MATERIALS

½ yard (.45 m) fashion fabric

½ yard lining material (bridal satin or taffeta)

½ yard interlining material (if fashion fabric is lightweight)

#9 millinery ribbon (its length head-size plus 1 inch)

1-inch-wide (2.5 cm) buckram strip, cut on the straight grain (its length head- size plus 2 inches, 5 cm)

Color-matched #24 basting thread and #50 sewing thread

Millinery ruler

#17 French curve

Four sheets of pattern paper, all 18-inch (46 cm) squares

Scissors, measuring tape, pencil, long metal-head pushpins, straight pins, #5 and #6 millinery needles

Headsize plate and balsa head block

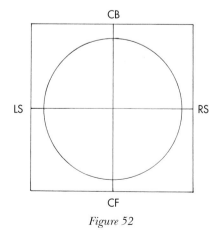

Figure 52

PATTERN DEVELOPMENT

❧ Fold each pattern paper square in half, then in half again to mark center. Unfold. Stack up all four sheets, matching centers. Using the millinery ruler or a compass, draw a 15-inch (38 cm) diameter circle on the top section. Draw a line through the center, marking CF and CB, and a second line across, marking LS and RS. (See Figure 52.)

❧ Cut out all four circles and number them consecutively—one, two, three, and four.

Circle #1: Facing

This circle will become a draft for the stylized facing of the beret, and gives the beret an interesting, attractive shape.

❧ Trace the headsize plate in the center of the circle, and mark CF, CB, LS, and RS. Allow for a ½-inch (13 mm) seam allowance around the headsize line. Adding the seam allowance around the headsize is tricky! You need to draw a new line that is ½ inch smaller than the actual headsize plate. (See Figure 53.)

❧ Cut through the headsize circle to the seam line in ½-inch intervals all around.

❧ Fit the circle over the balsa headblock the way you plan to wear the beret, and pin into the balsa along the headsize line. (See Figure 54.) Traditionally, the beret is worn tilted to one side. If you aren't certain, try finding such pictures in books and fashion magazines. Place the head block on a table where you will be comfortable and will have enough room to judge the "line" you want for the stylized beret.

❧ Have transparent adhesive tape or pins handy while slashing and shaping the beret. Using scissors, cut straight into the paper, almost to the headsize line. (See Figure 55.)

❧ Overlap the two sections and secure with tape. (See Figure 56.) The number of slashes and the degree of overlapping depend on the individual design. Overlapping the sections reduces the fullness of the material and gives it dimension Remember: **never** cut the center back line until the design is complete.

❧ Now review your design. Try the paper facing on your head, aligning the center front of the design with the center of your forehead. (Do this step carefully; the paper is now very deli-cate and tears easily.) Change or correct where needed. You can change the width of the facing by trimming it with scissors. (See Figure 57.) Train your eye to judge how much to cut. If you have removed too much, just tape some paper back on and re-do the line.

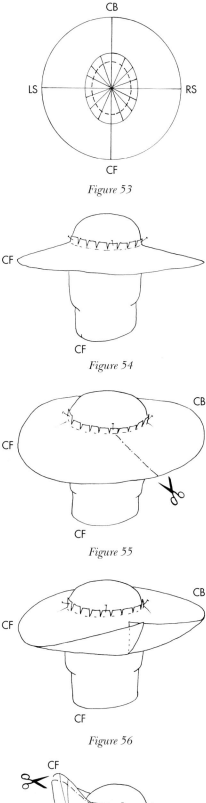

Figure 53

Figure 54

Figure 55

Figure 56

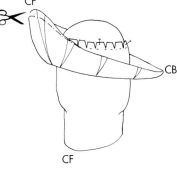

Figure 57

❧ Design Hint ❧

While you slash and overlap, keep in mind that the result should still resemble a somewhat flat beret. As a rule of thumb, if the sections overlap by more than ½ inch, the design will be too deep. Note that the goal of this process is to elim-inate all of the excess fullness you would see if this hat were a two-section beret.

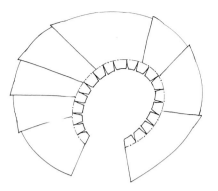

Figure 58

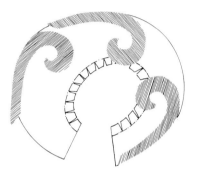

Figure 59

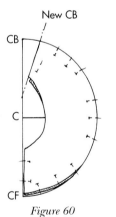

Figure 60

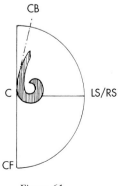

Figure 61

- When you are satisfied with the style, mark the center front, center back, and sides in different ink colors. Mark the center front line as the straight grain line. Now cut along the center back line.

  Pat the draft flat. Do not iron it!! (See Figure 58.)

- True the draft using a French curve, then trace it to a fresh pattern paper and mark it as "facing." (See Figure 59.)

Circle #2: Pointed Tip (Pagoda)

- Fold circle #2 in half along the front to back line.

- Fold the draft made from circle #1 in half, aligning with CB lines and pinning it along the outer edge until it becomes half of the original draft. Do not be concerned that the folded paper does not lie flat. After all the halves are not symmetrical. Also note that the original CF is no longer valid and a new center front has taken its place as a result of the slashing process.

- Pin the draft to the folded circle #2, aligning the center front fold lines and the outer edge of the draft to that of the circle. Circle #2 is larger than the draft. Mark the excess on the outer edge. Pencil a line along the CB line of the draft creating a V-shaped section that will likely end somewhere above the center of circle #2. (See Figure 60.)

- Using the French curve, connect the center point of circle #2 with the tip of the V in a slightly rounded line. When sewn, the result is a soft, pleasant tip rather than a sharp one. (See Figure 61.)

- Remove the draft from the circle, and cut out the V. This draft looks like a pizza pie that is missing a small slice. (See Figure 62.) Save the V section for the next design option.

- By bringing the V lines together, the circle becomes pagoda-like, and can be used as a tip for the beret. It should perfectly fit the facing pattern you made from circle #1. Mark this draft as "pointed tip" or "pagoda." (See Figure 63.)

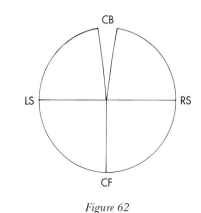

Figure 62

Figure 63

Circle #3: Four-Section Flat Tip

☙ Fold the V section lengthwise in half and then in half again so it is one quarter of the original size. (See Figures 64, 65, and 66.)

☙ Measure its widest section using a ruler or tape measure and write the measurement down. This measurement could be anywhere from ⅛ inch to ¾ inch (3 to 19.5 mm), depending on the size of the V gusset. For reference we will call this measurement X.

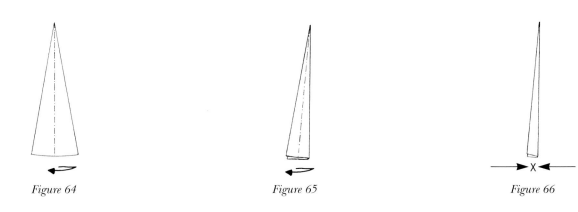

<table>
<tr><td>Figure 64</td><td>Figure 65</td><td>Figure 66</td></tr>
</table>

☙ Mark front-to-back and side-to-side lines on circle #3. Mark distance X on both sides of the center lines. The result, four identical small quarters, and each one should look like Figure 67.

☙ Cut one section along the new lines and mark the corner closest to the center of the circle with the letter C for center.

☙ Fold the section lengthwise and then lengthwise again. (See Figures 68 and 69.) You will notice a tiny excess along the outer edge of the section. Trim it off. (See Figure 70.) Leaving this excess in place results with a 'bump' in the final assembly.

☙ This piece will become a draft of a four-section top for the beret and as before should be a perfect fit to the stylized facing. Mark this draft as "four-section flat tip." (See Figure 71.)

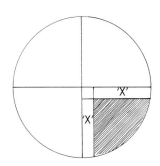

Figure 67

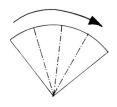

Figure 68

Figure 69

Figure 70

Figure 71

Circle #4: Flat Tip

Figure 72

Figure 73

- Fold circle #4 in half and then in half again, resulting in four quarters. (See Figure 72.) Make sure the folds are accurate and crisp.
- Take one of the three remaining sections of circle #3 and place it over the folded circle, aligning center and sides.
- Because the section from circle #3 is smaller, there will be excess at the edge. Cut off this excess from circle #4. (See Figure 73.)
- Unfold circle #4 to reveal yet another design option for the tip. Use this draft for the tip portion of the lining as well. Mark the draft as "flat tip."
- To turn these drafts into a working pattern, trace them onto a fresh sheet of pattern paper and add ½-inch seam allowance all around. (See Figures 74, 75, 76, and 77.)

∼· *Helpful Hint* ∼·

Mark each face of the "facing" pattern as "face" side and "hair" side so you can correctly place it on the fashion fabric when it's time to cut.

Figure 74

CUTTING ────────────────

- **Fashion Fabric:** Place the pattern so that the straight grain aligns with center front. If an interlining is needed, use it to back up the fabric and cut them as one.
- **Lining:** Use the one-piece circle and the stylized facing. Reduce the pattern by ¼ inch all around so that it will correctly fit into the beret.

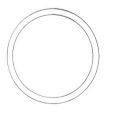

Figure 75

Figure 76

Figure 77

CONSTRUCTION

The stylized beret, whether plain, pagoda, or four sections, follows the same construction rules as the previous berets. The only difference is in the headband.

You can use the same band as you did in making the two-piece beret or an invisible one as described below.

❧ On the headsize line edge sew a piece of 5-inch (13 cm) bias tape made from French elastic or flexie. Flip the tape inside toward the lining. Sew in the sweatband (#5 or #9 millinery ribbon) slightly above the bias tape as in previous berets, overlapping in the back.

❧ Place the beret on the block and steam out any wrinkles.

❧ If the beret is rather large in diameter, slip a ring of steel wire into the widest part to support the shape after the hat is completed.

∼· *Design Hint* ∼·

The pagoda tip can look even more authentic not only by the choice of fabric, but also by adding satiny straps for tying under the chin or on the back of the neck. Just remember to angle the sewn ends.

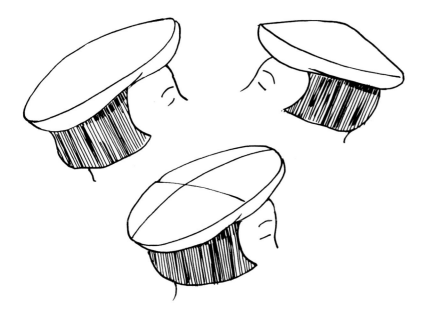

THE MULTI-SECTION BERET

THIS BASIC PATTERN CAN BE USED TO MAKE AT LEAST THREE DIFFERENT BERETS: AN EIGHT-SECTION BERET, A FOUR-SECTION BERET, AND A SINGLE-SECTION BERET. THERE ARE MANY VARIATIONS TO THE THEME AND A FEW ARE LISTED AT THE END OF THIS SECTION.

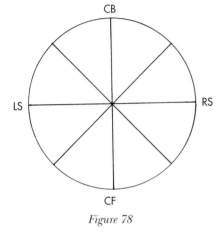

Figure 78

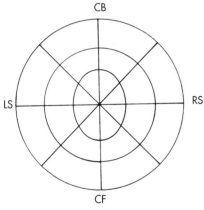

Figure 79

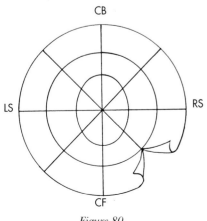

Figure 80

MATERIALS

½ yard (.45 m) fashion fabric

½ yard lining material (bridal satin or taffeta)

½ yard interlining fabric (if needed)

#9 millinery ribbon (headsize length plus 1 inch, 2.5 cm)

1-inch-wide buckram strip, cut on the straight grain (headsize length plus 2 inches, 5 cm)

color-matched #24 basting thread and #50 sewing thread

#5 and #6 millinery needles

One sheet pattern paper, 20 inches (50 cm) square

Millinery ruler

French curve No. 17

Scissors, measuring tape, pencil, long metal-head pushpins, straight pins,

Headsize plate and balsa headblock

PATTERN DEVELOPMENT

❦ Mark the center of the pattern paper square. Using the millinery ruler, draw an 18-inch (46 cm) diameter circle. Draw a line through the center and mark its ends as CF (center front) and CB (center back). Draw a second line through the center, across the circle (perpendicular to the first line), and mark its ends LS (left side) and RS (right side). Next, draw a through line bisecting the CF-LS section and another bisecting the CF-RS section. When finished, the marked-up draft should look like a pie, divided into eight sections. (See Figure 78.)

❦ Trace the headsize plate directly in the center of the circle, matching the front, back, and side markings.

❦ Measure the distance from the CF mark on the headsize plate to the edge of the draft. Divide it by half, and draw a circle that meets this half point. This circle indicates the circumference of the finished beret. (See Figure 79.)

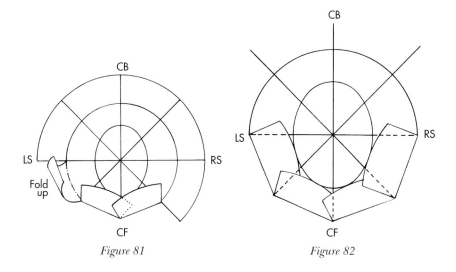

Figure 81	*Figure 82*	*Figure 83*

❧ Clip, using scissors, along the bisecting lines of all eight sections, but no farther than the outer edge of the middle circle. (See Figure 80.)

❧ Fold the outer sections onto themselves, making sure that they meet the headsize line. The side corners of the sections will overlap. (See Figure 81.)

❧ Trace the lines that are showing through the paper to the folded-over sections. (See Figure 82.) Unfold and transfer the traced lines from the back to the front of the draft. Cut off the 'triangular' excess. (See Figure 83.)

❧ Unfold the cut sections to reveal a teardrop shape. The eight "outer circumference" sections should add up to the headsize measurement. To find the individual section size, divide the headsize measurement by eight. For example: 22 inches divided by 8 = 2¾ inches (56 cm divided by 8 = 7 cm). Measure each section and adjust where necessary, either by enlarging or reducing the section. Complete the draft by using a No. 17 French curve to round the points on each section into a smooth curve. (See Figure 84.) Remove excess triangles around each section.

❧ Number each section to maintain its position on the draft. This practice is especially important if your fabric's design is asymmetrical or if you are using fashion fabric with nap.

The following are some of the ways you can use this versatile pattern:

~ 8 sections, use section #1 (See Figure 85.)

~ 4 sections, use section #s 1 and 2 (See Figure 86.)

~ 1 section, use entire pattern (See Figure 87.)

Note that the lining must be cut as a single section for best fit. Before transferring the pattern to the fabric, add a ½-inch (13 mm) seam allowance all around

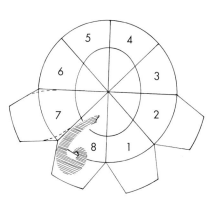

Figure 84

Figure 85

Figure 86

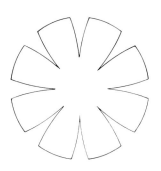

Figure 87

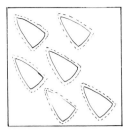

Figure 88

Figure 89

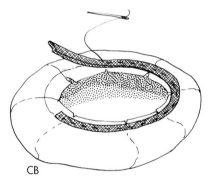

CB

Figure 90

CUTTING

For 8- and 4-section berets, cut all sections with the nap and grain in one direction. Refer to the position of each section on the original draft to determine grain direction. (See Figures 88 and 89.)

- ❧ If you need to use interlining fabric, cut it as a single unit with the fashion fabric.
- ❧ Cut the lining ¼ inch (6.5 mm) smaller than the fashion fabric.

CONSTRUCTION

- ❧ Matching the seam lines, sew the individual sections to each other, doing four sections at a time. Press the seams open using a steam iron and a pressing roll .
- ❧ Baste the large sections to each other, starting from the pointed top, making sure that all sections correctly meet at the center.
- ❧ Sew the lining together and fit it into the beret, matching the seam line and grain direction of the beret and the lining.

Headband: There are two options for a headband.

1. A headband made from a separate section as for the two-piece beret.
2. No visible headband but rather a finished edge done as described below.
   - ❧ Sew a 1-inch-wide French elastic strip along the seam allowance of the headsize line, slightly below the seam line. (See Figure 90.)
   - ❧ Turn the seam allowance into the hat along the seam line and hand sew #9 millinery ribbon in the same manner used for the previous berets.
   - ❧ Place the finished beret on the balsa block, steam away any wrinkles, and allow to thoroughly dry.

❧· *Design Hint* ·❧

Trim with self-fabric trim, beads, flower(s), or a bow, or attach a visor. Other ways to create an interesting look include shirring or pleating the sections to the headsize band without rounding them first; shifting the headsize plate off center during the pattern development stage; dividing the circle to five, seven, or nine sections; making the sections uneven in width; and using different colors and textures for each section. Topstitching is another pretty addition to solid color hats.

THE VISOR

A SIDE FROM BEING VERY FUNCTIONAL, A VISOR ADDS FUN AND STYLE TO CASUAL HEADWEAR. USE CONTRASTING COLORS, ASSYMETRICAL DESIGNS, SCALE, AND SIZE TO ADD INTEREST TO A BASIC DESIGN. THE FICTIONAL DETECTIVE SHERLOCK HOLMES WORE A HAT WITH VISORS AT BOTH FRONT AND BACK! THINK OF A VISOR AS A PARTIAL BRIM AND LET YOUR IMAGINATION ROLL. TRY ADDING VISORS TO ANY OF THE BERETS IN THE PREVIOUS CHAPTERS.

MATERIALS

½ yard (.45 m) fashion fabric

½ yard stiff buckram

16-inch (41 cm) square of pattern paper

Millinery ruler

#17 French curve

#24 basting thread and #50 sewing thread

Scissors, self-adhesive transparent tape, pencil, pushpins, straight pins, needles

Balsa headblock and headsize plate

PATTERN DEVELOPMENT

- Trace the headsize plate at the marked center of a pattern paper sheet and mark CF, CB, LS, and RS.
- Measure ⅜ to ½ inch (9.5 to 13 mm) above the cross line (LS-RS), and draw through this point a line parallel to the former one. Mark the new point NLS and NRS. These new points are located just behind the ears, where the visor's pointy sides should end. (See Figure 91.)
- To establish the width of the visor, place the ruler at CF and measure 4 inches (10 cm) down. This point is the edge of the visor. However, the visor can be as narrow or wide as you wish
- Using the millinery ruler, draw a circle around the headsize from this point. Cut out the circle. Slash the headsize like a starburst in ½-inch increments. (See Figure 92.)
- Fit the circle over the headblock, and pin along the headsize line. Place the headsize block on a table where you will be comfortable and will have enough room to judge the "line" you want for the visor.
- Have self-adhesive tape handy while slashing and shaping the visor. Begin by cutting, using scissors, straight into the paper,

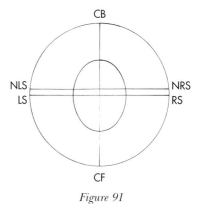

Figure 91

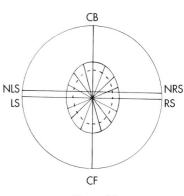

Figure 92

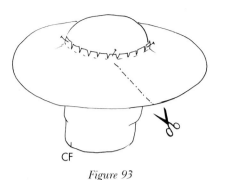

Figure 93

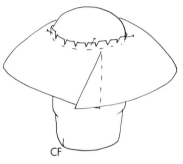

Figure 94

almost to the headsize line. (See Figure 93.) Overlap the two sections and secure with tape. (See Figure 94.) Just as in the stylized beret, the number of slashes and the degree of overlapping depend on the individual design. Remember: **Never** cut the back line until the design is complete.

- A visor is really only a partial brim, so use scissors to reduce its size. Train your eye to guide you in cutting a pleasing visor shape freehand. Start cutting at the CF and end at NRS and NLS. (See Figure 95.)

- When designing a visor, divide it into two imaginary halves: left and right. Once you have finished the construction, select the more interesting side and discard the other.

- Now review your design. Change or correct where needed. Choose the side of the visor that is preferred, and discard the other.

- Pat the draft flat. Do not iron!!

- True the draft using a French curve. Trace it on to fresh pattern paper if desired and mark its identification.

- Trace the selected half on a folded sheet of pattern paper, aligning the center front on the fold. When unfolded, the draft becomes a complete, symmetrical pattern. (See Figure 96.)

CUTTING

- Add seam allowance to the pattern and trace it on to the fashion fabric. You will need two pieces: one for the top, cut on straight grain, and the other for the bottom facing, cut on the bias. (See Figure 97.)

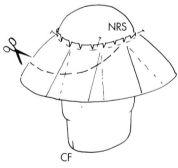

Figure 95

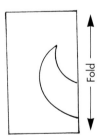

Figure 96

Figure 97

Making a Stiff Foundation Insert

- Trace the draft (without seam allowance) onto stiff buckram. Cut out two identical pieces.
- Place a moist kitchen towel over the buckram. Using a steam iron, press both pieces together until they bond.
- For washable hats I prefer using Timtex™, a new synthetic stiff material. (See Source List.)

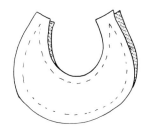

Figure 98

CONSTRUCTION

- Sew the top and bottom sections together to create a pocket; turn it inside out. (See Figure 98.)
- Slip the stiff buckram foundation insert into the pocket, making sure it fits perfectly. (See Figure 99.)
- Stitch close along the headsize seam line.

ASSEMBLING THE VISOR TO THE HAT

- Match the center fronts of the hat and the visor. Pin them together, starting at the center and working your way to the side, one section at a time. (See Figure 100.)
- Add some ease at the side portion. Use your judgment about the ease. The amount depends on the hat's design and fit. Never try to fit a visor before the hat is at its final stage of completion.
- Sew in the visor either by hand with a strong backstitch or by machine.
- Sew in the sweatband (millinery ribbon #5 or #9) as for all other hats.

Variation: Attach the visor to a 1-inch (2.5 cm) headband instead of attaching it directly to the crown.

Insert

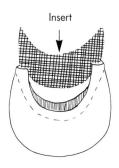

Figure 99

Figure 100

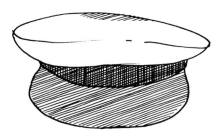

*Figure 101
with band*

*Figure 102
without band*

THE CLOCHE

THE CLOCHE IS A PERENNIAL FAVORITE! HERE WE WILL MAKE IT AS A TWO-PART HAT—A CROWN AND A SHORT BRIM. THE CROWN IS MADE UP OF SECTIONS, USUALLY FOUR, SIX, OR EIGHT, BUT SOMETIMES MORE. FASHION TRENDS MAY DICTATE SHORTER OR DEEPER CROWNS. WHATEVER DEPTH YOU CHOOSE, THE CLOCHE SHOULD FIT SNUGLY AND BE PROPORTIONAL TO THE WEARER'S HEAD SIZE, FACE, AND FIGURE.

MATERIALS

1 yard (.9 m) fashion fabric

1 yard lining fabric

1 yard interlining fabric

Pattern paper

No. 17 French curve

Millinery ruler

Pressing roll

Scissors, measuring tape, needles, straight pins, long metal-head pushpins

Balsa headblock and headsize plate

～ Helpful Hint ～

Complete the pattern development for both the crown and the brim before beginning the cutting and sewing process.

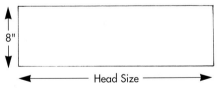

Figure 103

Figure 104

CROWN PATTERN DEVELOPMENT

❧ Cut out a paper strip measuring 8 inches (20 cm) wide with the length determined by headsize measurement. (See Figure 103.)

❧ Divide the paper into even sections by folding it. For a six-section crown, for example, fold the strip of paper in half, then in thirds. (See Figures 104 and 105.) For an eight- section crown, fold the paper in half, then in quarters. (See Figures 106, 107, and 108.) If you want an odd number of sections, divide the length of the paper by the number of sections, mark them with a pencil, and fold along the marks. The dotted line indicates the center of the section where you make the last fold.

❧ Measure and mark up 3 inches (7.5 cm) from the edge where the multiple folds show. This is the forehead mark; this section should be almost straight. (See Figure 109.)

❧ On the French curve, measure 1 inch (2.5 cm) down from the narrow end and mark this point on the ruler. (See Figure 110.)

❧ Place the marked point on the upper corner of the single-fold side and connect it to the 3-inch mark with a gradual curved line. (See Figure 111.)

❧ Cut along the curved line through all paper thickness while still folded. When unfolded, you will have a multisection crown draft. These sections combined will equal the headsize measurement. (See Figure 112.)

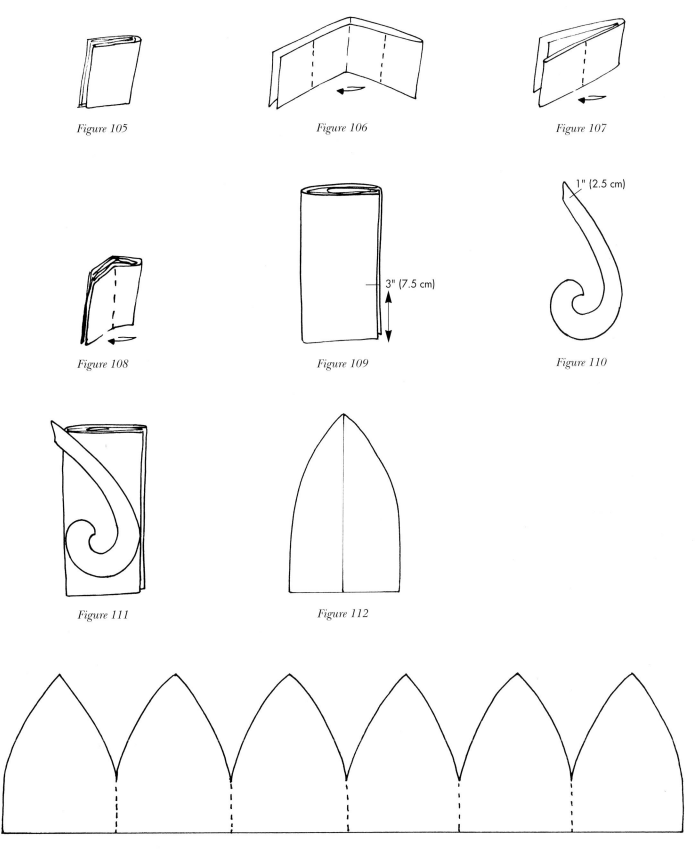

Figure 105

Figure 106

Figure 107

1" (2.5 cm)

3" (7.5 cm)

Figure 108

Figure 109

Figure 110

Figure 111

Figure 112

Figure 113

Variation: For a single-piece crown with multisections on the tip portion, repeat all of the fold steps shown above. Cut along the curved edge only, but do not separate the sections. (See Figure 113.)

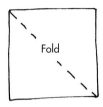

Figure 114

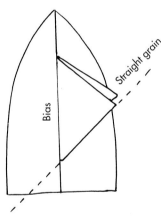

Figure 115

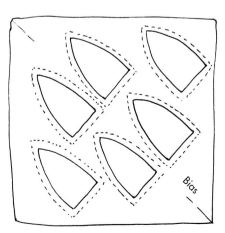

Figure 116

- Mark the grain direction on the pattern. The true bias line connects the tip point and the center bottom section (the headsize line), and the straight grain is 45° on the diagonal of the true bias line.
- Label each draft with the proper headsize and mark the straight grain direction. Remember that a seam allowance has not yet been included.
- Add seam allowance to the pattern. Note that the seam allowance needs to be adjusted to the weight and type of the fabric, and to the method of construction used. For example, thicker fabric may require a wider seam allowance; curved lines and tapered or pointed corners may require a narrower seam allowance. It is important to determine these needs before proceeding, so practice cutting using scrap material.

CUTTING

- Before moving on, consider the following questions. Will the materials, both fashion fabric and lining, hold up to normal usage? The lining should be either taffeta or bridal satin. Both hold up very well.

  Is the fabric heavy enough on its own, or does it need the support of interlining?

  How does the fabric feel? Bunch it up and see how it stands on the table. If it doesn't stand by iteself, it will probably need a backing material such as taffeta, muslin, crinoline, flalean, or French elastic. Sometimes the lining material will provide just enough support without the need for a layer of interlining. Allow yourself to experiment with different material combinations.

Warning: Do not use fusible interlining!! It tends to bubble and pucker in heat and humidity and will ruin your hard work.

- Trace both the seam line and the seam allowance line onto the wrong side of the fabric, aligning the grain line. Remember that the center line, from tip to base, marks the true bias on each pattern piece. All patterns should point to the same direction, especially when using fabric with nap. (See Figure 116.)
- Cut fashion fabric, lining, and interlining (if needed).

CONSTRUCTION

Sewing the crown

- Perform the following steps for fashion fabric and lining. If interlining is needed, handle fashion fabric and interlining as a single unit.
- Starting from the tip, match and baste three sections at a time (half the crown) along the curved seam line. Before basting the sections, secure the point at the tip where all sections meet with a ⅛-inch (3 mm) backstitch or a pin. Locking the point

firmly is important for all multisection crowns.

- Pin the crown pieces together at the center. To make a perfect center point, stick a pin through the center tip of the crown. Be sure the seams lie flat and face opposite directions on both sides of the pin. Let both the point and the head of the pin project through so that you can be certain that the points exactly match. (See Figures 117, 118, and 119.)

    This is one of the most important steps in making a multi-section crown. Often, due to inexperience or the need to "cut corners," a trim is added to the center in order to camouflage the fact that the points do not meet.

- Before machine stitching the seams, remove about 2 inches (5 cm) of the basting stitches that join the two crown halves at the tip where all the sections meet, taking care not to fray the fabric. Removing the stitches makes machine stitching the next four seams much easier.

- Sew both halves by machine. Do not sew above the place where the pointed tips meet. Tie the stitching threads on the wrong side of the fabric.

- Use your thumbnail to flatten the seams open. If you are using a velvet fabric, the seams must be steamed instead of pressed.

- After perfectly connecting the center tips, finish sewing the section downward to the headsize line. Complete the remaining section in the same manner and finger press the seams open.

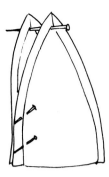

Figure 117

Figure 118

Blocking the Crown

- Slip the sewn crown over the balsa block and pin at the head-size line. Mark the CF and CB of the crown. The crown should fit tightly, without wrinkles. If it does not, make any necessary alterations such as adding or removing extra fullness. If you alter one seam, do it to all seams, otherwise the sections will be uneven.

- Baste any pinned alterations and reblock the crown.

- It is best to block and press the crown on the balsa headblock. Mark the center front and back using a thread in contrasting color, turn the crown with the seam allowance facing out, and place over the block to press the seams open and flat. Remove from the block and set aside.

Blocking the Lining and Crown

- Place the lining on the balsa block with right side toward the block and wrong side facing out, matching the front, back, and sides with those of the block. (See Figure 120.)

- Working gently but firmly, thoroughly steam the lining and smooth it down to conform to the block. Pin the edges to the block to prevent the fabric from creeping back up.

- Place the fabric crown with wrong side facing the block over

~· Helpful Hint ·~

To correctly sew a crown, you must work from the top down for all sections, no matter how many. The result is always a professional looking crown.

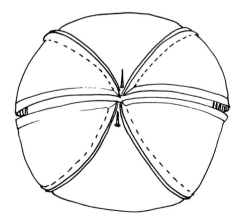

Figure 119

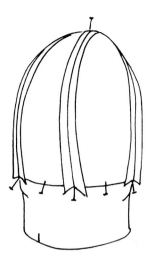

Figure 120

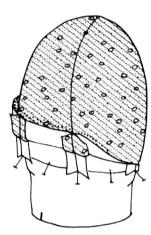

Figure 121

~· **Advanced Tip** ·~

Cut the brim free hand to achieve an effect like that shown in Figure 127, where the brim is longer at the front and shorter at the back.

the lining, matching the seams, center tip, front, back, and sides. (See Figure 121.)

- Thoroughly steam the fabric crown and smooth it down to conform to the block as you did before. Pin all around to prevent layers from shifting.
- Leave the crown on the block while working on the brim.

BRIM PATTERN DEVELOPMENT

- Trace the headsize plate in the center of a pattern paper. Mark the CF, CB, LS, and RS.
- Measure out 3 inches from center front; through this point draw a circle on pattern paper using the millinery ruler. (See Figure 122.)
- Cut out the circle. Allow for ½-inch (13 mm) seam allowance around the headsize line. Cut through the headsize circle to the seam line in ½-inch intervals all around. (See Figure 123.)
- Fit the brim over the balsa head and pin along the headsize line.
- Begin by cutting, using scissors, straight into the brim, almost to the headsize line. (See Figures 124 and 125.)
- Overlap the two sections and secure with transparent tape. The number of slashes and the degree of overlapping depend on the individual design. Remember: Never cut the center-back line until the design is completed. (See Figure 126.)
- Now review your design. Often one side looks more pleasing than the other. Mark the CF, CB, and sides in different ink colors. Mark the center front line as the straight grain line. Cut along this line and along the center back line. Keep the section you liked most and discard the other.
- True the brim draft using a French curve. Then trace it to a fresh pattern paper folded in half. Place the CF line along the fold, so you'll get a full brim at once. (See Figure 128.) Mark CF, CB, LS, RS, and grain direction. Add ½-inch seam allowance where needed. (See Figure 129.)

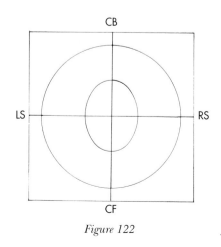

Figure 122

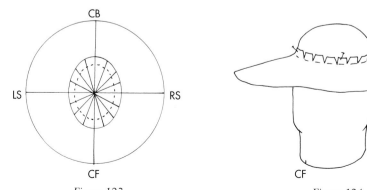

Figure 123

Figure 124

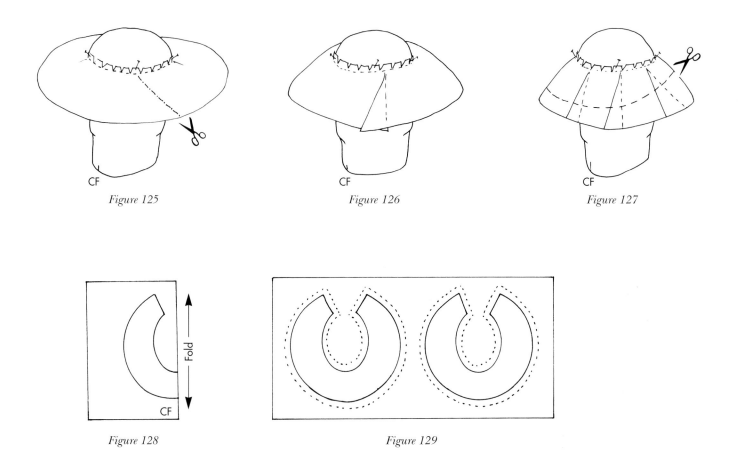

Figure 125

Figure 126

Figure 127

Figure 128

Figure 129

CUTTING

- Cut two pieces for the brim, a top facing and a bottom facing that mirror each other. When cutting, either double the fabric, matching right sides together, or cut a single layer with the pattern facing up and a second layer with the pattern facing down.
- Choose interlining based on how stiff you want the brim to be. Do not use fusible interlining!! Try any of the following: interfacing used in tailoring (sold under several brand names, I use Hymo), French elastic, Flexie, any nonfusible interlining (found in sewing-supply stores)
- Cut the interlining only once using the same brim pattern. Mark the top and bottom sides on the cut section!

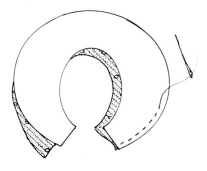

Figure 130

CONSTRUCTION

- Match both fabric brim sections, right sides together.
- Place the interlining section on the top facing section.
- Align all sections perfectly and baste along the seam line. (See Figure 130.)
- Hand or machine stitch.
- Press the sewn edge flat. If it seems too bulky, trim the interlining or one of the fabric layers as close to the seam as possible.
- Align and stitch the back seam. (See Figure 131.)

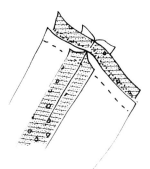

Figure 131

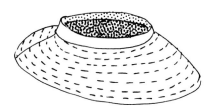

Figure 132

Figure 133

- Press the seam open and turn brim inside out.
- Press the brim firmly. If desired, topstitch around the brim with a sewing machine. Always stitch from the outside in. (See Figure 132.)

ASSEMBLING THE CROWN AND BRIM

- BEFORE you assemble the crown and brim, test their fit and design. Place the crown on the balsa block and add the brim. Measure how deep you'd like the crown to be, then carefully pin the brim to the crown. (See Figure 133.)
- Try the hat on your head. Does it look right? Make any adjustments now. Transfer the final details to the crown pattern so you can duplicate the fit on the next hat .
- Trim any excess fabric below the brim line.
- Stay stitch around the cut edge of the crown to ensure all layers stay together.
- Combine the crown and brim in one of the illustrated methods. Stitch the two together securely. The first two methods depend on the kind of trim or absence of one; the third one is generally used for rain hats. (See Figures 134, 135, and 136.)
- Sew in the sweatband using #9 millinery ribbon as in previous hats.

TRIMMING

Trim the crown with a bias strip of the hat fabric or with #5 or #9 millinery ribbon, hiding the row ends with a bow.

Figure 134

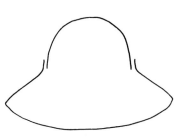

Figure 135

Figure 136

RIGID
FRAME
HATS

THE PILLBOX

T HE PILLBOX IS A SMALL HAT WITH AN UPRIGHT SIDE BAND AND A FLAT TIP. IT IS MADE BY COVERING A STIFF FOUNDATION FRAME WITH A FASHION FABRIC, AND GOT ITS NAME FROM ITS RESEMBLANCE TO OLD-FASHIONED PILLBOXES. THE HAT'S STYLE DATES AS FAR BACK AS ANCIENT GREECE, WHERE WOMEN ADORNED THEIR PILLBOX HATS WITH FOUR TULIPS TO ANNOUNCE AN ENGAGEMENT, AND THE FLOWERS WERE BELIEVED TO BE POWERFUL LOVE TALISMANS. MORE RECENTLY, THIS HAT STYLE WAS MADE POPULAR IN THE EARLY 1960s BY THEN FIRST LADY JACQUELINE KENNEDY.

MATERIALS

1 yard (.9 m) fashion fabric

1 yard stiff buckram or flexie

1 yard lining material

Bias strip of French elastic or seam binding tape

#19 covered frame wire*

#24 basting thread

Pattern paper

Scissors, pencil, straight pins, needles

Millinery ruler

Headsize plate

Important: Millinery frame wire comes coiled and it is essential to take the spring out of the wire before using it. With thumbs of both hands, gently but firmly stroke the wire against the back of the curve. The wire will become straighter, allowing you to reshape it to the desired contour.

PATTERN DEVELOPMENT

Tip (the top part of the hat)
- Mark the center of a 9-inch (23 cm) square sheet of pattern paper either by measuring or by folding the sheet in half twice.
- Center the headsize plate on the paper. Trace it and mark center front (CF), center back (CB), and sides (LS, RS). (See Figure 137.)

Side Band
- Draw a rectangle on pattern paper the length of the headsize and the width to suit your design. (The traditional width is between 3 and 4 inches, 7.5 and 10 cm.) (See Figure 138.)

Helpful Hint

Human heads are not round but oval, elongated from front to back. For a perfect fit, always follow the headsize plate.

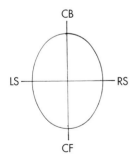

Figure 137

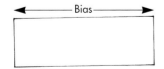

Figure 138

CUTTING

Foundation Frame

- Trace the tip pattern and markings on stiff buckram.
- Trace the side band on the true bias of flexie or buckram and add 2 inches (5 cm) to the length on each side. This excess will be overlapping when the back is sewn.
- Cut out both pieces and set aside.

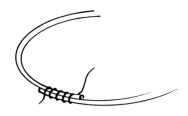

Figure 139

> ### ⌁· *Helpful Hint* ·⌁
>
> Frame material is generally sold off a roll, which makes the piece you work with roll in a certain direction. It is best to work with the roll direction and not to force it the other way.

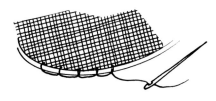

Figure 140

Fashion Fabric

- Tip: Cut 9-inch square piece of fashion fabric.
- Sideband: Cut a bias strip of fabric using the foundation frame pattern with ½-inch (13 mm) seam allowance added all around.

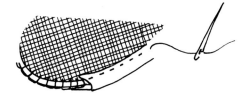

Figure 141

CONSTRUCTION

Foundation Frame Tip

- Measure the tip circumference, plus 3 inches for overlapping and cut a piece of #19 wire to that length. (See Figure 139.)
- Using a #24 thread and a ⅜-inch (10 mm) buttonhole hand stitch, sew the wire along the edge, overlapping the ends at the back. (See Figure 140.)
- Bind the wired edge with bias strip of French elastic. (See Figure 141.)

Foundation Frame Side Band

- Join the side band at the back, sewing it by hand (small backstitch) or sewing machine.
- Again, measure the tip circumference, plus 3 inches for overlapping, and cut a piece of #19 wire to that length.
- Sew #19 wire along the top edge of the band and bind with French elastic bias strip as described above.
- Sew #21 wire along the bottom edge of the side band and bind with French elastic band as well.
- Matching front and back markings, join the tip and side band using an overcast hand stitch. Make sure the needle penetrates all material thicknesses to ensure a strong bond. (See Figures 142 and 143.)

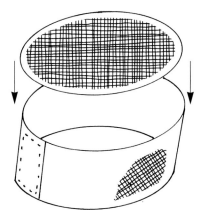

Figure 142

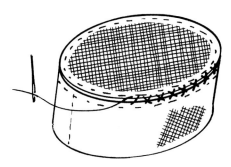

Figure 143

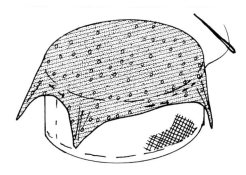

Figure 144

~· **Helpful Hint** ~·

Unless stitches are a decorative
element in the design of the hat,
they should be invisible.

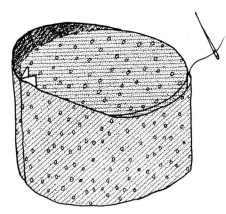

Figure 145

COVERING THE FRAME

Tip

- Place the fabric square on the tip, aligning the straight grain from front to back, and pin in place.
- Pull and draw the fabric tautly over the edge of the flat surface, and pin it about ½ inch below the edge, on the side band. It is easier if you coax opposite corners into place first, and then work with the sides. (See Figure 144.)
- Hand-stitch the edges to the side band using a long backstitch. Trim off excess fabric.

Side Band

- Join the band at the back by hand or sewing machine. Open the seam with your fingers. Do not press open, as ironing will press the bias out of shape.
- Carefully slip the sewn side band over the frame, matching the back seam with center back of the foundation frame.
- Smoothly drape the fabric all around the frame
- Turn under ½ inch for seam allowance and slip stitch to the fabric covering the tip. (See Figure 145.)
- Turn excess fabric under the headsize edge and stitch to the frame only.

Lining

- Cut and sew the lining using the same pattern used for the frame with the following two exceptions. First, the pattern pieces need to be ¼ inch (6.5 mm) smaller all around. Second, add a ½-inch seam allowance all around.
- Once the lining is sewn, press the seams flat and insert it into the hat, matching center front and back. It should fit snugly without any excess or shortage of material.
- Hand stitch the lining around the head size.
- Finish off with sewing in a sweat band as for previous hats.

Design Variations

- Increase the width of the side band to create horizontal pleats.
- For the side band, use several narrower bias strips, crossing them at either the front or back.
- Trim with bows, flowers, or attach a veil.

THE BOATER

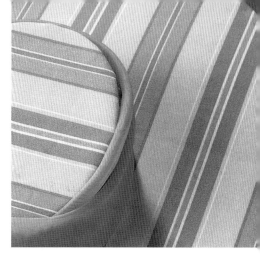

THIS UNCOMPLICATED LOOKING, FLAT-CROWNED, HARD-BRIMMED STRAW HAT HAS BEEN A PERENNIAL FASHION STAPLE SINCE THE 1700S WHEN SAILORS WOULD BRAID THE STRAW THEMSELVES. ALSO CALLED A "SAILOR," THE BOATER IS EASILY MADE BY ADDING A FLAT BRIM TO A PILLBOX.

MATERIALS

Basic pillbox frame, 3 to 4½ inches deep (8 to 11 cm)

18-inch (46 cm) square of stiff buckram

Steel wire* and a wire joiner

#21 covered millinery wire

Bias strip of French elastic or seam binding tape

Sewing notions

Millinery ruler

Headsize plate

*CAUTION: Steel wire tends to spring back to a straight position. Always protect your eyes with safety glasses when handling and cutting steel wire!!

CROWN

Cover pillbox following the guidelines described in the Pillbox chapter.

BRIM

BRIM PATTERN DEVELOPMENT

- ❧ Place the headsize plate at the marked center of the buckram sheet and trace it. Mark CF, CB, LS, and RS.
- ❧ Establish the width of the brim by measuring it from the center front point of the headsize to the edge of the brim. The brim can be as narrow or wide as you wish.
- ❧ Using the millinery ruler, draw a circle around the headsize, matching the brim width. The resulting brim will be wider at the sides and narrower at the front and back, conforming to the oval shape of the head. To the viewer, the roundness of brim will seem proportionately correct. If you wish to have an even brim all around, do so by measuring that distance all around the headsize. (See Figure 146.)
- ❧ **Before cutting, add a ½-inch (13 mm) seam allowance to the headsize. Remember, adding seam allowance at the headsize line really means that you will be cutting out an oval ½ inch smaller than the actual headsize.**

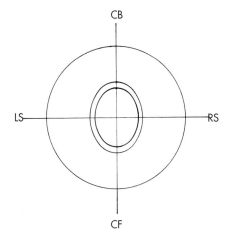

Figure 146

83

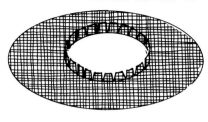

Figure 147

CUTTING

⚑ Cut excess buckram around the brim and remove the appropriate amount from the center. Slash the seam allowance at ½-inch intervals and bend the sections upward. (See Figure 147.)

CONSTRUCTION

⚑ Cut the steel wire to the circumference size of the outer edge of the brim and connect the ends with a wire joiner. (See Figures 148 and 149.)

⚑ Using a buttonhole stitch, sew the wire to the outer edge of the brim. Place the wire joiner at the back. (See Figure 150.)

⚑ Apply the #21 covered wire around the headsize, overlapping the ends 3 inches at the back.

⚑ Use 1-inch-wide (2.5 cm) bias French elastic band to bind the raw edges of the brim. (See Figure 151.)

⚑ Sew the same band over the wire at the headsize.

> ⌣· **Helpful Tip** ·⌣
>
> Measure the steel wire with great accuracy. If it is too long or too short the brim will be distorted!.

Figure 148

Figure 149

COVERING THE FLAT BRIM FRAME WITH FABRIC

> ### MATERIALS
>
> 1 yard (.9 m) fashion fabric
>
> 1 yard lining material
>
> Steel wire and a wire joiner
>
> Sewing notions

CUTTING

⚑ To cover the brim, use the brim pattern to cut two identical brim section out of fashion fabric. This time, remember to add a ½-inch seam allowance to the outer edge of the brim. You will later fold it under itself to hide the raw edge.

Figure 150

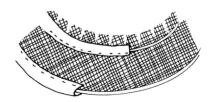

Figure 151

COVERING BOTTOM FACING

- Pin the top facing piece to the frame, making sure it is smooth and wrinkle free.
- Fold the seam allowance over the outer edge of the brim and stitch only to the buckram all around. Use a modified overcast stitch as shown. (See Figures 152 and 153.)

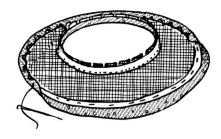

Figure 152

COVERING THE TOP FACING

- A fabric-covered brim requires two brim wires, with both facings—top and bottom—perfectly aligned and balanced.
- Pin the bottom facing piece to the frame, making sure it is smooth and wrinkle free. Let the seam allowance extend over the brim's edge.
- Measure a piece of steel wire that is as long as the brim circumference and connect the ends with a metal joiner.
- Place the joint about 2 inches (5 cm) away from center back to prevent bulk.
- Hold this wire loop against the first one and start turning the bottom facing's seam allowance over the wire. (See Figure 154.) Use the narrowest seam allowance needed to maintain a smooth edge. Excess may show thorough.
- Continue to fold and pin the seam allowance over the wire all around the brim.

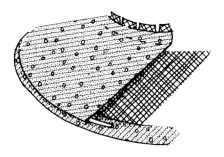

Figure 153

Caution: Stitching can be tricky, so carefully study the instructions before beginning.

- Hold the frame in one hand and the threaded needle in the other. With slight pressure, drag the needle along the bottom side of the wire to mark a groove. This groove will be the guide to a straight stitch line.
- Insert the needle below the wire and pull it out at the top and through the seam allowance of the top facing. Insert the needle through the seam allowance again and pull it at the marked groove line below the wire. (See Figure 155.)
- Make your stitches even and small, about ⅛ to ³⁄₁₆ inch (3 - 6 mm) long.
- Secure the headsize with a long backstitch.

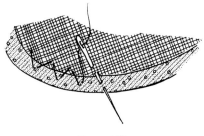

Figure 154

JOINING THE CROWN AND BRIM

- Place the pillbox over the brim's collar and join with a strong backstitch. Insert the lining into the crown and apply the sweatband as for all hats.

Figure 155

COVERING A BOATER FRAME WITH STRAW BRAID

COMMERCIAL BRAIDS ARE MADE BY AUTOMATED MACHINES THAT WEAVE AND PLAIT INDIVIDUAL STRANDS OF RAFFIA, STRAW, OR MAN-MADE MATERIALS (PLASTIC, PAPER, FIBERS). THEY ARE SOLD IN BUNDLES AND AVAILABLE IN MANY COLORS, WIDTHS, AND TEXTURES. TODAY'S POPULAR SEWN STRAW HATS ARE MADE ON MACHINES DESIGNED ESPECIALLY FOR THIS TASK, AND SKILLED PROFESSIONALS CAN EASILY PRODUCE 20 HATS A DAY ON THESE MACHINES. THE FOLLOWING HAND-SEWN TECHNIQUE YIELDS A FIRMER HAT THAN ONE MADE BY MACHINE.

MATERIALS

1 bundle of straw braid* (Choose one at least ½ inch, 13 mm, wide or you'll be hand sewing forever!!!)

Buckram boater's hat frame (brim and crown separated)

Matching thread

Straight pins

½ yard (.45 m) lining material

#9 millinery ribbon for the sweatband

*Dry, stiff straw can be softened by wrapping it up in a wet towel for a few hours to make the straw pliable and less brittle. Synthetic braids do not need special preparations.

Figure 156

Figure 157

Figure 158

CONSTRUCTION

- All straw braids have a thread running lengthwise along the outer edge. If you pull it out gently, the end of the braid will coil around itself. Pull a little more and it will start forming a flat spiral disc. (See Figure 156.) This is where the crown starts, at the center top.
- Wrap the extra length of the thread around the braid end to prevent it from unraveling. (See Figure 157.)
- Tuck the end under the first curve and fasten with needle and thread.
- Start curving the braid around going counterclockwise. The upper edge of each new turn should go under lower edge of the previous one. (See Figure 158.)

~ *Helpful Hint* ~

Shape the spiral so it is not a perfect circle, but conforms to the oval shape of the tip.

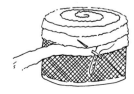

Figure 159

- After the third row or so, place a pressing cloth over the circle and press it with a steam iron. Take the opportunity to swirl the next 15 inches (38 cm) using the same technique you would use in swirling a ribbon. This will make the braid lie perfectly flat as you continue the construction of the tip.
- Now start inserting the needle through the buckram and braid as you continue to build out the tip.
- Once the tip is covered, start working down the side band. First pin the braid around the side band, then sew it as before, again inserting the needle through the buckram.
- Continue pinning and sewing until the side band is completed, then tuck the end under the last row. (See Figures 159 and 160.)

Figure 160

Covering the Brim's Top Facing

- Start from the outer edge of the brim and work your way toward the headsize collar. As you sew the first row, let the braid overhang about ¼ inch (6 mm), thus covering the wire edge of the frame. (See Figure 161.)

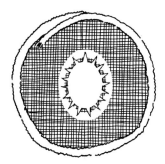

Figure 161

> ᴠ·*Helpful Hint*·ᴠ
>
> If the brim is not a perfect circle, you will have to make adjustments similar to the ones you have used in covering the tip. For example, you may need to "ovalize" the overlap of rows to conform to the shape of the brim, especially as you get closer to the headsize collar.

- Start covering the bottom facing of the brim. Line the first row with the outer edge of the top facing, then proceed with pinning and sewing through all layers up to the headsize collar.
- Be careful not to continue sewing the straw into the headsize collar, or the hat will end up too small.

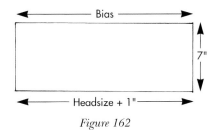

Figure 162

FRENCH LINING

- Measure a bias strip of lining material the length of the headsize with a ½-inch seam allowance added. Its width should be approximately 7 inches (18 cm). Rule of thumb: The width is about the height of the side band plus half of the tip's diameter. (See Figure 162.)
- Sew the strip to form a band. (See Figure 163.)
- Whipstitch along the edge of one open end and pull the thread until the opening gets very small. (See Figure 164.)
- Turn the lining to the wrong side and cover the opening with a patch of the same material. Stitch in place. (See Figure 165.)
- Place lining over the balsa head and press with a steam iron. Fit the lining into the crown, aligning the back seam with the crown's center back. Stitch the lining to the crown along the bottom edge (headsize), and trim off excess material.
- Finish the hat by sewing in the sweatband, covering all raw edges of straw braid and lining.
- If desired, add a bow or a flower to complete the design.

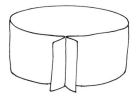

Figure 163

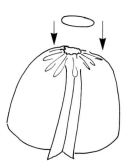

Figure 164

DESIGNING RIGID FRAMES

Designing rigid frames is like creating a sculpture. Stiff buckram and wired edges allows you to construct complex shapes that maintain their integrity through wear and use. A dramatic profile hat with a very large brim can stop a crowd in its tracks!

MATERIALS

- 20-inch (50 cm) square of fashion fabric (medium-weight fabrics; e.g., wool jersey, cotton, suiting, velvet, bridal satin, brocade)

- #24 basting thread and #50 sewing thread that matches the brim's fabric

- 1 yard stiff buckram

- Bias strip of French elastic or seam binding

- 20-inch square of pattern paper

- #17 French curve

- Millinery ruler

- Pins and self-adhesive transparent tape, scissors

- Balsa headblock and headsize plate

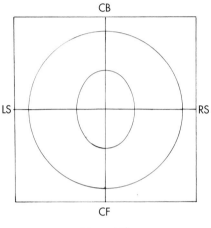

Figure 165

STYLIZED BRIMS

Stylized brims are designed using the same slash-and-shape method you learned for the stylized beret, the cloche, and the visor.

PATTERN DEVELOPMENT

- Trace the headsize plate at the marked center of the pattern paper sheet. Mark CF, CB, LS, and RS.

- To establish the width of the brim, place the ruler at CF and measure 4 inches (10 cm) down. This point is the edge of the brim. The brim may be as narrow or wide as you wish, but 4 inches is a good starting width.

- Using the millinery ruler draw a circle around the headsize from this point. (See Figure 165.)

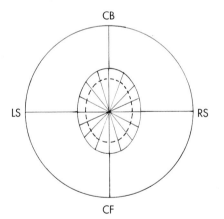

Figure 166

- Cut out the circle. Slash the headsize like a starburst in ½-inch (13 mm) increments. (See Figure 166.) This circle will become a draft for the stylized brim.

- Fit the circle over the headblock, and pin along the headsize line. Place the head- size block on a table where you will be comfortable and will have enough room to judge the "line" you want for the stylized brim. (See Figure 167.)

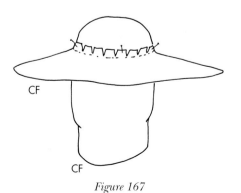

Figure 167

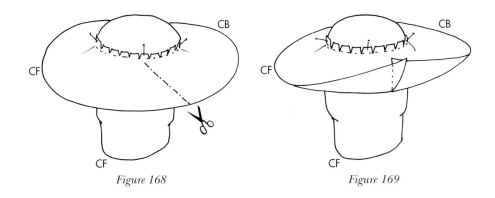

Figure 168   Figure 169   Figure 170

🍂 Have self-adhesive tape handy while slashing and shaping the brim. Begin by cutting, using scissors, straight into the paper, almost to the headsize line. (See Figure 168.) Overlap the two sections and secure with tape. (See Figure 169.) The number of slashes and the degree of overlapping depend on the individual design. Remember **never** to cut the back line until the design is complete.

~· *Design Hint* ·~

Two flattering brim styles include the roller, where the brim is turned up symmetrically on all sides, and the profile brim, where the brim is turned up on one side only (front, back or side). When designing a roller, divide the brim into two imaginary halves—left and right. Once you have finished the construction, select the more pleasing side and discard the other. Then place the center front line along a fold line of a pattern paper sheet and carefully trace. Unfolded, the sheet reveals a complete pattern. The profile brim, being asymmetrical, is styled as a single unit.

🍂 Review your design. Try the paper brim on your head, aligning the center front of the design with the center of your forehead. (Do it carefully; the paper is now very delicate and easily tears.) Change or correct where needed. You can change the width of the brim by trimming it with scissors. (See Figure 171.) Train your eye to judge how much to cut. If you have cut too much, just tape some paper back on and re-do the line.

🍂 Mark the center front, center back and sides in different ink colors. Mark the center front line as the straight grain line. Cut along the center back line.

🍂 Pat the draft flat. Do not iron it!! (See Figure 172.)

🍂 True the draft using a French curve, then trace it onto a fresh pattern paper if desired and mark its identification. (See Figure 173.)

~· *Advanced Design* ·~

For a special waved or pleated effect, slash the brim and add a triangle of paper. After wiring the frame, bend and pleat this section to your design. (See Figure 170.)

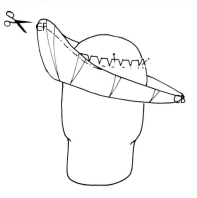

Figure 171

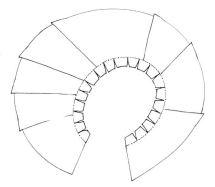

Figure 172

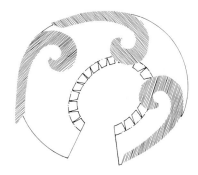

Figure 173

89

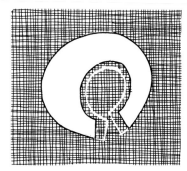

Figure 174

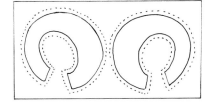

Figure 175

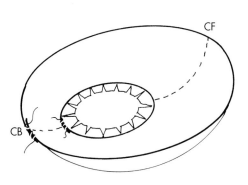

Figure 176

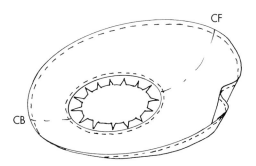

Figure 177

CUTTING

Frame

❧ Trace the pattern onto buckram adding a 1-inch (2.5 cm) collar around the headsize and an additional 2 inches (5 cm) to each end of center back for overlap. (You do not need to add a seam allowance around the buckram brim.) Mark the center back line on each end so overlapping is accurate! (See Figure 174.)

Fashion fabric

❧ Trace the pattern onto the fabric twice—once for the top facing and once for the bottom facing. Before cutting the fabric, check the layout. The top facing should be a mirror image of the bottom facing!! Fabric grain direction should align with CF. Align the two if your fabric has nap or special pattern. Add seam allowance all around. (See Figure 175.)

FRAME CONSTRUCTION

❧ Join the frame at the back by overlapping the 2-inch ends and securing with a strong stitch.

❧ Measure #19 wire to fit the circumference of the brim and add 4 inches (10 cm) for overlap.

❧ Join the ends and align the overlap with the center back of the frame.

❧ Apply the wire to the brim edge using a buttonhole stitch; bind the edge with a 1-inch bias strip of French elastic, just as you did for the boater brim. (See page 85.)

❧ Apply #19 wire to the headsize in the same manner. (See Figure 176.)

❧ Style the brim to match the paper pattern you have developed. If one side of the brim was turned up, so should the buckram frame.

~· *Advanced Design Hint* ·~

At this point you could also bend the brim wire into the pleats or scallops (shown in Figure 170) for an added dimension. (See Figure 177.) Such details require an experienced hand and are difficult to cover with fabric.

COVERING THE FRAME

❧ This part is almost identical to covering a boater frame, but there is one major difference. Here you are dealing with an asymmetrical, three-dimensional shape, making it a challenge to balance the top and the bottom facings. The merit of using two wires is most evident in this process. Stretchy jerseys or velvets are easiest to handle when covering such frames.

❧ Start by covering the facing that is least visible to the eye. If the brim is turned up, start with the top facing; conversely, if the brim is turned down, as in a mushroom shape, start with the bottom facing.

FIRST FACING

- Pin the first facing piece to the frame. Start at the CF and work around to the CB on one side and then the other. Make sure it is smooth and wrinkle free. If the fit is right, you should have a ½-inch seam allowance left at the CB.
- Where the surface is curvy, it will be necessary to tack the fabric to the buckram frame. Thread a needle with a thread color matched to the fashion fabric. Tack the fabric to the frame using tiny stitches, going around the brim in a large zigzag pattern as used in tailoring. (See figure 178.) The stitch must not be visible at all on the fabric side.
- Let one end lie flat on the brim and fold the other seam allowance under itself, aligning it with the CB. Use a slip stitch to secure it in place. (See Figure 179.)
- Fold the seam allowance over the outer edge of the brim and stitch to the seam binding only all around. (See Figure 180.)

SECOND FACING

- Prepare a loop of #21 wire the length of the brim's circumference plus 3 inches (7.5 cm) for overlap. Join the ends securely as described before.
- Pin the second facing piece to the frame, making sure it is smooth and wrinkle free. Let the seam allowance extend over the brim edge.
- Place the wire joint about 2 inches away from the center back to avoid bulk buildup.
- Holding the second wire loop against the first one, start turning the bottom facing's seam allowance over the wire. (See Figure 181.) Use the narrowest seam allowance needed to maintain a smooth edge. Excess may show through.
- Continue to fold and pin the seam allowance over the wire all around the brim.
- As in the flat boater brim, stitching can be tricky, so study the instructions carefully before beginning.
- Hold the frame in one hand and the threaded needle in the other.
- With slight pressure, drag the needle along the bottom side of the wire to mark a groove. This groove will be the guide to a straight stitch line.
- Insert the needle below the wire and pull it out at the top through the seam allowance of the top facing. (See Figure 182.)
- Insert the needle through the seam allowance again and pull it at the marked groove line below the wire.
- Make your stitches even and small, about ⅛ to ³⁄₁₆ inch (3 - 5 mm) long. Smooth the facing down over the brim and secure the headsize line with a backstitch.

Read on about Simple Blocked Crowns suitable for the stylized brims.

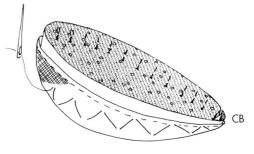

Figure 178

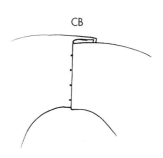

Figure 179

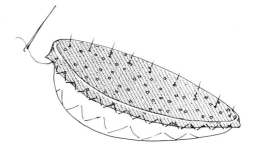

Figure 180

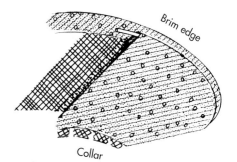

Figure 181

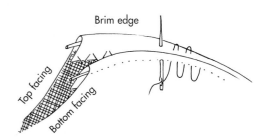

Figure 182

SIMPLE BLOCKED CROWN FOR COVERED FRAMES

THE STYLIZED BRIM IS THE DOMINANT DESIGN ELEMENT FOR THIS TYPE HAT. A SIMPLE CROWN IS ALL IT NEEDS.

MATERIALS

15-inch (38 cm) square of fashion fabric

15-inch square of lining fabric

15-inch square of flexie or buckram

Bias strip of French elastic or seam binding

Elastic band, ½ inch (13 mm) wide and long enough to fit snugly around the headblock, its ends joined in a loop

Scissors, measuring tape, needles, straight pins, long metal-head pushpins

Balsa headblock

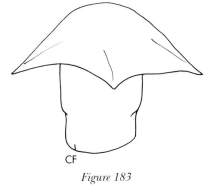

CF

Figure 183

CONSTRUCTION

Lining Fabric

❧ Drape the lining material over the headblock, aligning the grain with the CF and CB. (See Figure 183.)

❧ Secure the fabric to the block with pushpins and elastic band. (See Figure 184.)

❧ Apply steam to the fabric and coax it into shape by pulling and twisting its opposite corners. (See Figure 185.)

❧ Secure with pushpins and remove elastic band. (See Figure 186.)

Foundation Fabric

❧ Drape the buckram or flexie over the headblock, aligning the grain with the CF and CB.

❧ Secure the buckram to the block with pushpins.

❧ Apply steam to the buckram, and coax buckram into shape by pulling and twisting its opposite corners.

❧ Secure with pushpins.

CF

Figure 184

Fashion Fabric

❧ Drape the fashion fabric over the headblock, aligning grain with CF. Secure the fabric to the block with pushpins and elastic band.

❧ Apply steam to the fabric, and coax fabric into shape by pulling and twisting its opposite corners.

❧ Secure with pushpins. Let dry completely before continuing. (See Figure 187.)

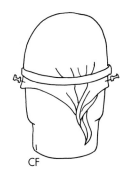

CF

Figure 185

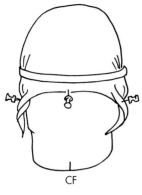

Figure 186

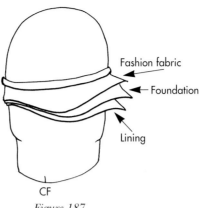

Fashion fabric

Foundation

Lining

Figure 187

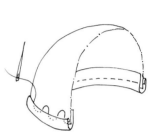

CF

Figure 188

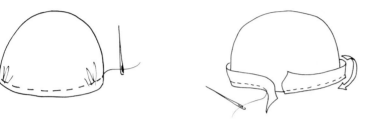

Figure 189

Figure 190

Figure 191

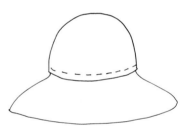

Figure 192

- Use the top edge of the elastic band to mark with a tailor's chalk the desired depth of the crown. Clearly mark CF, CB, RS, and LS
- Cut along the bottom edge of the elastic band through all fabric thickness with a sharp craft cutting blade. (See Figure 188.)
- Remove the crown from the block by carefully loosening and easing the sides up.
- Preserve the headsize dimension by backstitching close to the edge through all layers. (See Figure 189.)
- Trim excess material below the seam line. No seam allowance is needed for this crown.

It is best to cover the raw edge with a bias strip. Place the strip on the outside of the crown and stitch along the edge. Turn over the raw edge and stitch in the ditch. (See Figures 190 and 191.)

ASSEMBLING THE CROWN AND BRIM —

1. Crown Over Brim (See Figure 192.)
- Cover the raw edge with a ribbon trim or bind it as described above. Stitch the crown and brim with a strong backstitch.

2. Brim Over Crown (See Figure 193.)
- Cover the raw edge of the crown with a bias binding as described above. Place the brim over the crown and securely stitch. Trim the raw edge of the brim's headsize with a self-fabric drape or ribbon trim. Finish off by inserting a sweat-band as for all hats.

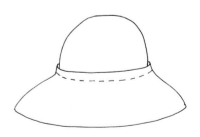

Figure 193

TURBANS

TURBANS

Turbans impart the mysterious, alluring flavor of the Far East, weaving the subtle spell of the Orient. Turbans look deceptively complicated, yet are quite easy to make. They can be symmetrical (like an Eastern turban) or asymmetrical; they can be deep or shallow; they can cover both ears or just one; and they can be accentuated with a variety of textures created from creative drapes, pleats, and gathers. Turbans can be made from featherweight fabrics for summer, or from warm and woolly fabrics for winter (even draped over a felt crown for extra warmth). All turbans follow one principle: start with a form-fitting cap (the foundation), and then drape fabric over it. The secret to a well-made turban is a well-placed drape and minimal sewing and tucking. The draped fabric must look as if it is held together by nothing at all.

THE BASIC TURBAN

The basic turban is light, attractive, and practical. A carefully draped yard of pretty fabric can project sophistication, and effectively cure even the worst case of bad-hair-day.

MATERIALS

1 yard (.9 m) fashion fabric (challis, jersey, and crepe de Chine make good choices. Keep in mind that very sheer or lightweight fabrics must be backed with a heavier interlining fabric such as muslin or flalean. Without backing, these fabrics will not have enough body and covering power.)

15-inch square (38 cm) French net If you do not have French net, dip a piece of heavy-duty lace in sizing (millinery gelatin, regular gelatin, spray starch, diluted craft stiffener). Let dry completely and proceed as with the French net.

#9 millinery ribbon

Straight pins, thread, needles, scissors

Clear plastic bag

Balsa headblock for draping

MEASURING

- Measure the head circumference to determine headblock size needed and then measure the following (see Figure 194).
- Determine how deep (#1) from the base of the neck to the forehead the turban will fit on the head.
- Measure ear to ear (#2). Decide now if you want the earlobes covered or not.
- Measure around the head (#3) especially if there's a full head of curls with a measuring tape, slipping one finger under the tape for ease.

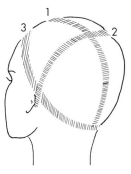

Figure 194

CB

Figure 195

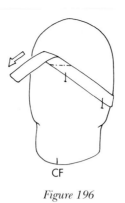

CF

Figure 196

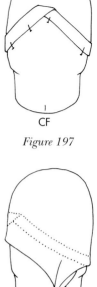

CF

Figure 197

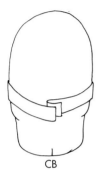

CB

Figure 198

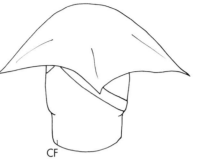

CF

Figure 199

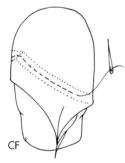

CF

Figure 200

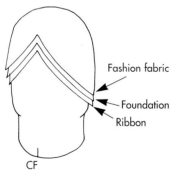

CF

Figure 201

Fashion fabric

Foundation

Ribbon

CF

Figure 202

❧ Mark all measurements on the balsa block.

FOUNDATION CONSTRUCTION

❧ Cover the balsa block with a protective plastic bag.

❧ Fold back ½ inch (13 mm) of #9 ribbon and anchor it (raw end facing out) to the center back of the block with a straight pin. (See Figure 195.) Bend the pin downward.

❧ Snugly wrap the ribbon around the block, pinning it along the measured marks and bending the pins flat down.

❧ Cross the ribbon at the front as shown. (See Figures 196 and 197.) Continue wrapping and pinning until you reach center back again.

❧ Extend the ribbon ½ inch beyond the center back point and secure with a stitch. (See Figures 198.)

❧ Inspect your work. Where there's extra fullness in the ribbon (particularly around the ears), tuck small pleats with a cross-stitch.

❧ Drape French net or stiffened lace over the block with the straight grain running front to back. Pin CF, CB, LS, and RS. (See Figure 199.)

❧ Apply steam (with a steam iron or steamer) and gently pull the corners, twisting and pinning them down as you work. (See Figure 200.)

❧ Stitch the French net through the ribbon with a backstitch (long stitch on top and short stitch on the bottom). (See Figure 201.)

❧ Remove the pins from the French net and trim any excess material close to seam line.

❧ Drape a 15-inch square of fashion fabric on top of the net layer with the straight grain along the front to back line. Pin down at the CF, CB, LS, and RS.

- Steam as you did with the net, pulling and twisting the corners until the fabric is as smooth as possible. (Note: When using knit or other stretchy material, do not stretch excessively or the turban will end up too small.)
- With color-matched thread, backstitch the fabric through both net and ribbon.
- Remove the pins from the French net and trim excess material close to the seam line.
- The foundation is now completed. (See Figure 202.)

DRAPING

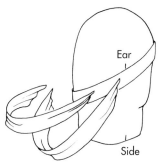

Figure 203

- Cut two bias strips 9 - 15 inches (23 - 38 cm) wide and 5 - 6 inches (13 - 15 cm) longer than the headsize. If the fabric is very fine (e.g., crepe de Chine) back it up with light muslin to provide body and support. Cut lightweight material 4 - 5 inches (10 - 13 cm) wider than one with the body.
- Stitch the sharp end of one bias strip at the back of the right ear mark. (See Figure 203.)
- Stitch down the end of the second bias strip at the half point between the first strip and center back. Place under the first strip.
- While draping, keep folding the raw edges of the strip under, creating a neat edge.
- Start draping clockwise, crisscrossing the strips as you work. You should have about four crossings by the time you reach center front. To keep the authentic look of a turban, position one crisscross at the center front. (See Figure 204.)
- Continue to drape and cross until you have run out of fabric (typically, around center back).
- Finally, tuck the ends underneath the drape hidden from view. (See Figure 205.)
- Examine your design. Now is the time to reshape gathers and pleats. Force yourself to start over if necessary.

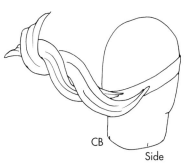

Figure 204

FINISHING

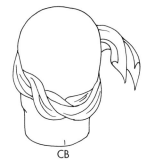

Figure 205

- Finely crafted turbans look as if the wrap naturally holds itself in place. Underneath, completely invisible stitches securely hold the turban together and maintain the original design.
- Using color-matched thread, start stitching on the inside of the drape and through the crown fabric. Pay special attention to securing the crisscrossed intersections.
- Stitch through the pleats in a large zigzag stitch. (See Figure 206.)
- Steam well to set the design, and dry completely while still on the block. If in doubt, let it dry overnight. Drying is critical because this style is form-fitting and any shrinking could hurt the fit.
- Remove the turban from the block and slip stitch the headsize ribbon to the fabric, securing the outer edge.
- Trim with knots, bows, or feathers for a dramatic focal point.

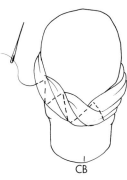

Figure 206

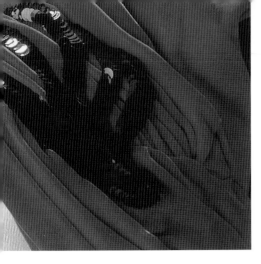

BUILT-UP TURBAN

LIKE THE BASIC TURBAN, THE BUILT-UP TURBAN STARTS WITH A FORM-FITTING CAP, BUT THIS IS WHERE THE SIMILARITY ENDS. WHEN YOU'VE FINISHED YOUR FIRST BUILT-UP TURBAN, YOU WILL REALIZE THAT IT'S A RELATIVELY RIGID STRUCTURE, WITH THE TAILORED FEEL OF A HAT.

MATERIALS

1¼ yards (1.1 m) fashion fabric (challis, jersey, and crepe de Chine fabrics work well. Very sheer or lightweight fabrics must be backed with a heavier interlining fabric. Without backing, these fabrics do not have enough body and covering power.)

1 yard long x 5 inches (13 cm) wide strip of flexie cut on a true bias

15-inch (38 cm) square lining material

1 yard (.9 m) flexie

#9 millinery ribbon

Straight pins, thread, needles, scissors

Balsa headblock for draping

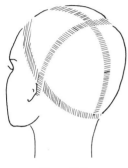

Figure 207

FOUNDATION CONSTRUCTION

- Measure the head, following the same directions as for the basic turban and transfer the measurements to the balsa headblock. (See Figure 207.) Plan the silhouette and line of the design. With the built-up construction, you can let your imagination loose because the firm padding added to the foundation allows you to sculpt any shape imaginable.

- Identify the true bias direction of the fashion fabric. Measure and cut a 6-inch-wide (15 cm) bias strip with its length being the measurement of the head wrap plus 6 inches.

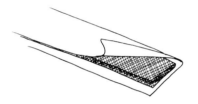

Figure 208

- Fold the 5-inch-wide strip of bias-cut flexie in half and encase it in the bias strip of fabric you have just made. (See Figure 208.)

- Fold the strip lengthwise, make a crisp crease, and mark the halfway point. This is the center back (CB). (See Figure 209.)

Figure 209

- Align the strip's center back to the corresponding point on the balsa headblock with the folded (closed edge) side facing out. (See Figure 210.)

- Guiding both ends toward the center front and following the depth measurements of the ears and center back, shape, pull, and urge the band to conform to the contours of the head, pinning as you work.

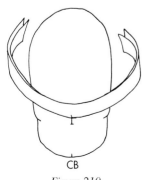

CB

Figure 210

- Overlap the ends at the center front and stitch securely. (See Figure 211.)
- Sew the raw edges of the band in long backstitches (long stitches underneath and small ones on top) all around the head, pulling slightly to smooth and remove any bulk or fullness. (See Figure 212.)
- Trim excess fabric all around the band.

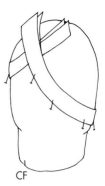

Figure 211

Lining
- Drape the lining material over the block with the grain straight to the CF. Using gentle steam, smooth the material over the block, pulling opposite corners, twisting them, and securing with pins. (See Figure 213.)
- Sew through the lining to the band in long backstitches (long stitches on top and small ones on bottom) all around the head, pulling slightly to smooth and remove any bulk or fullness. (See Figure 214.)
- Trim excess fabric ½ inch (13 mm) away from the seam line.

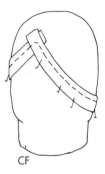

Figure 212

Foundation
- Cut a 15-inch square of flexie and drape it over the lining with the grain straight to the CF.
- Repeat the same steps as for the lining.

Tip
- Cut a 15-inch square of the fashion fabric and drape it over the lining with the grain straight to the CF.
- Repeat the same steps as for the foundation.

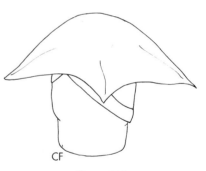

Figure 213

DRAPING

While you could easily drape a bias strip of fabric around the foundation as you did to the basic turban, why not do something really wild over this firm and solid structure? For example, build a raised shape made of flexie and cover it with fashion fabric, create double or triple tiers of flexie bands, an asymmetrical twist, or anything else your imagination conjures up. Let's explore the double-tier example.

Double-Tier Drape Construction
- Prepare three bias strips of the fashion fabric, one measuring 19 x 5 inches (48 x 13 cm), one measuring 20 x 5 inches (50 x 13 x cm), and another the length of two wraps around the head and 5 inches wide. Set the longest strip aside.
- Prepare two bias strips of flexie, one measuring 19 x 3 inches (48 x 7.5 cm) and one measuring 20 x 3 inches (50 x 7.5 cm).
- Cover the flexie strips with corresponding strips of fashion fabric and gently fold lengthwise, creating a soft and rounded

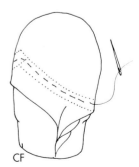

Figure 214

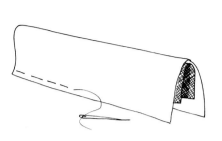

Figure 215

Figure 216

Figure 217

Figure 218

Figure 219

Figure 220

~· Advanced Design Hint ·~

To save time, mount a small pill-box on top of the foundation and drape over and around it.

crease. Baste along the raw edge to hold the two edges together. (See Figure 215.)

☙ Next, build up the strips on the foundation. Start by bending the shorter strip into a crescent shape and placing it on the block. Study the balance and design. Is it too far to the back? Is it too tall? Adjust as necessary and hand stitch the raw edges to the foundation with a strong back stitch. (See Figure 216.) Bend the longer strip into a crescent shape too. Place it just below the first one, while covering the first strip's raw edge. Again, once you are satisfied with the design, secure the strip to the foundation as with the shorter strip. (See Figure 217.)

☙ Now start draping the longer bias strip around the head, making sure that all the raw edges are concealed. (See Figures 218, 219, and 220.)

☙ Secure the drape as you did for the basic turban, stitching through the pleats in a large zigzag through-stitch.

☙ Steam well to set the design and let dry completely while still on the block. If in doubt, let it dry overnight. Drying is critical because this style is form-fitting; any shrinking could hurt the fit, making the hat fall apart.

☙ Once the turban is dry, remove from the block and finish by stitching the band to the draped edge.

☙ Inside, cover any showing stitches with a strip of pretty lace. Insert a sweatband as you would for all hats.

SPECIAL OCCASION HATS

THE COCKTAIL HAT

THESE LITTLE "SWEET-NOTHINGS" MAKE STYLISH MOOD-SETTERS AND MAKE A GREAT FASHION STATEMENT AT SPECIAL OCCASIONS SUCH A COCKTAIL PARTIES AND WEDDINGS. WORN TILTED FORWARD OVER THE EYES, THEY NEED HELP FROM A COMB OR THIN ELASTIC CORD TO STAY ON. COCKTAIL HATS CAN BE DESIGNED TO COMPLEMENT A SPECIAL OUTFIT BY SUING THE SAME FABRIC AND COMMON ELEMENTS OF STYLE.

MATERIALS

1 yard (.9 m) fashion fabric

12-inch (30 cm) square of cape net or heavily sized lace or buckram

30- x 2-inch-wide (75 x 5 cm) bias strip of flexie

Bias strip of French elastic or seam binding tape

Clear plastic bag (large enough to cover the headblock)

#19 covered wire

Twill tape or # 1 ribbon

Pushpins, straight pins, thread, needles

½-inch-wide (13 mm) elastic band, long enough to fit snugly around the headblock, its ends joined to form a loop

A water bottle with non aerosol spray pump

Balsa headblock

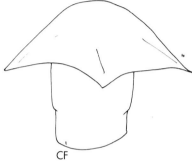

CF

Figure 221

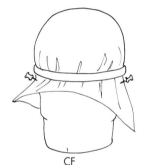

CF

Figure 222

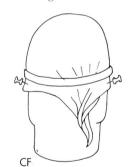

CF

Figure 223

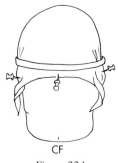

CF

Figure 224

CONSTRUCTION

- Place the plastic bag over the headblock to protect it.
- Lightly mist the cape net (or stiffened lace) with water using the spray pump.
- Steam the cape net and drape over the block, lining the grain along front to back. (See Figure 221.)
- Anchor the cape net to the block with pushpins and slip the elastic band over it. (See Figure 222.) Continue steaming; tug and pull the corners of the material only until it is wrinkle-free and conforms to the headblock shape. (See Figures 223 and 224.)

REMEMBER: This hat is going to be quite small, so do not overstretch the material. Also, wash your hands frequently; stickiness from the moist sizing can soil your fashion fabric.

- Place a 12-inch square of fashion fabric over the cape net, aligning the straight grain front to back.
- Place the elastic band over both the fabric and the cape net.
- Pull, tug, and smooth the fabric. Note: It's easier to remove the wrinkles if you pull in the bias direction, corner to corner.

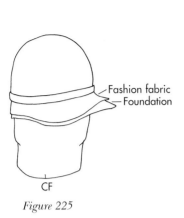

Figure 225

Figure 226

Figure 227

- Steam well.
- Continue smoothing the fabric until it is completely wrinkle-free in the area above the elastic band. Stick pushpins into the fabric's edge to hold it in place during drying.
- Steam well again. All the steaming will make the sizing act as an adhesive, practically bonding the fabric to the cape net.
- Set the headblock aside until completely dry. (See Figure 225.)

General Recommendations

- When using cape net, there's no need for lining.Cape net is pleasing to the eye.
- Using buckram requires lining. Refer to Easy Blocked Crowns on page 92. There, you place the lining material on the block, followed by the buckram, and finally the fashion fabric. Follow the same steps for this hat.
- Avoid using sheer fashion fabric. If you must, add a solid inter-lining so the foundation material will not show.

Figure 228

DESIGN

- The shape of the cap is entirely up to you. Choose from classic shapes such as the Juliet (Figure 226), side-to-side crescents (Figure 227), or teardrops (Figure 228) to freehand irregular shapes. It's easier to master the classic shapes and then move on to more challenging designs.
- Have a piece of twill tape or very narrow ribbon and a few pins handy.
- Mark the center front (CF) and center back (CB) on the fabric with a pin or contrasting thread.
- Study the headblock and chose a starting point to pin the ribbon to the block.
- Use the ribbon as a marking tool, drawing it across and around the block, pinning down if needed, until the shape pleases you. (See Figure 229.) (Instructions continued on page 106.)

Figure 229

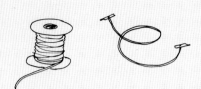

Figure 230

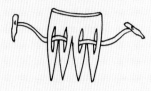

Figure 231

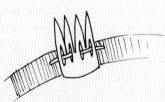

Figure 232

Figure 233

Figure 234

KEEPING COCKTAIL CAPS ON

There are many methods for keeping small cocktail caps on. Here are three of the most common ones. Experiment with them all since wearers often prefer one method over another.

TUBULAR ELASTIC CORD

❧ Tubular cording can be purchased by the yard or precut with metal stays at its ends. It is available in either black or white. The white elastic can be custom-dyed with permanent felt tip pens. If you use the elastic with metal stays, just insert the stays through the sweatband ribbon and lock them in place. Otherwise, thread the elastic through a large-eyed needle and tie a big knot at each end to secure. (See Figure 230.)

THE COMB

❧ Small plastic combs are best purchased in clear or brown so they blend with any hair color. Begin by breaking a six-teeth section off the comb. This is all the comb width you will need; anything wider will be too noticeable. Study the hat and decide where to place the comb. Sometimes a single, well-positioned comb is enough. Generally, two combs positioned at opposite sides of the head are needed.

❧ Measure and cut a 4-inch (10 cm) length of tubular elastic, with or without metal stays. Thread the cord through the comb's closed loops. (See Figure 231.) Insert each end through the sweatband and secure with a knot on the other side. Do not stretch the elastic; rather let it remain loose. (See Figure 232.)

❧ To place and fasten the combs, grip the combs by the end closest to the sweatband. (See Figures 233 and 234.) Suspend the hat about an inch (2.5 cm) above the head, and at the same time pull the combs in opposite directions, carefully stretched away from each other.

❧ Still maintaining the stretch, turn the combs' teeth toward the scalp and let them penetrate the hair. Give a gentle but firm push to the combs (teeth now facing the hat) until you feel the resistance of the hair. This is the sign that the hat is well anchored.

❧ Practice these steps until you have them mastered.

Figure 235

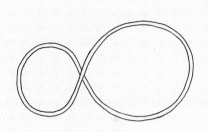

Figure 236

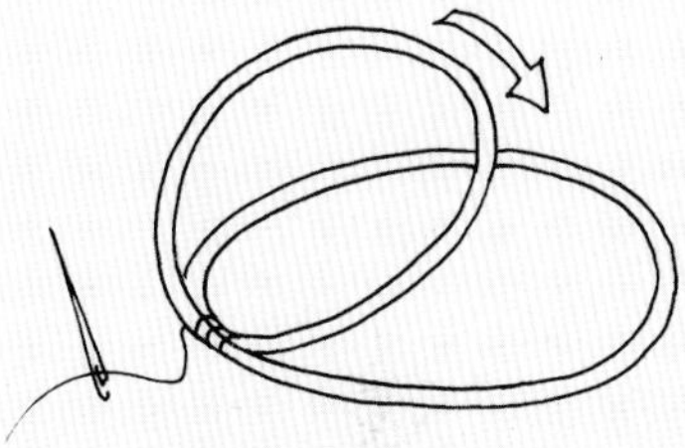

Figure 237

THE FIGURE EIGHT

- Cut a piece #19 wire to twice the length of the headsize. Cover the wire with ribbon tubing, wraps of veiling, or with a velvet bias strip, choosing a color close to the wearer's hair color so it will be less noticeable. Join the wire ends to a loop, overlapping about 3 inches (7.5 cm) and securing with tie wire. (See Figure 235.) Neatly join the wrapping ends.

- Twist the loop, forming a figure-eight shape, then collapse it to form a small loop within a larger loop. The larger loop should fit the headsize perfectly, while the smaller loop keeps the hat on the head. (See Figure 236.)

- Stitch the point where the loops cross each other. During use, this intersection will be under a lot of stress, so make sure the stitches will hold!! (See Figure 237.)

- Place the large loop just below the crown edge, aligning the intersection to the center back. (See Figure 238.) Stitch the large loop to the crown using a pick stitch.

- To place and fasten the figure-eight loop to the head, hold the hat with one hand and the small loop with the other hand. Separate them gently and feel the spring tension. Place the hat on top of the head and let the small loop clamp it to the back of the head. If needed, you can bend the small loop to conform to the wearer's head. (See Figure 239.)

Figure 238

Figure 239

CF

Figure 240

Figure 241

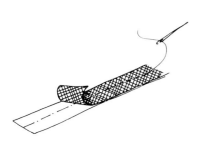

Figure 242

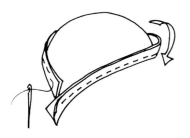

Figure 243

❧ Baste through all material layers along the bottom edge of the ribbon to both mark the shape on the fabric and to ensure that all layers stay together. (See Figure 240.) Use a craft knife to cut out the shape right below the basting stitches.

❧ Attach #19 wire to the edge of the shape, bending the wire to conform to the contour. Use a buttonhole stitch and overlap 3 inches (7.5 cm) of the wire edges at the center back. If the center back is pointed, overlap the wire along a straight portion of the shape. (See Figure 241.)

❧ Cover the wire on the wire edges with bias strips of French elastic or bias tape.

FINISHING

❧ Cut a 2-inch-wide (5 cm) bias strip of fabric (self fabric is always a safe choice) long enough to fit the circumference of the cap plus 5 inches.

❧ Place the bias strip over the 2-inch-wide flexible strip and baste along the center. (See Figure 242.)

❧ Line up the raw edge of the band with the wired edge of the cap, starting at center back if the design allows. (See Figure 243.)

❧· Helpful Hint ·❧

If the design includes a point, begin sewing at the pointed edge and end at the same place. This guarantees a perfectly defined tip.

❧ Stitch ½ inch away from the edge all around the cap.

❧ Trim off any excess strip length, leaving just enough to fold under itself for a neat finish.

❧ Flip the ribbon over the wire edge toward the bottom of the cap.

❧· Helpful Hint ·❧

Avoid bulky layers! Trim off any excess fabric or foundation material that is not going to be visible.

❧ Secure the overlap of both strip ends with a few stitches, then continue stitching the raw edge to the wire binding.

❧ Finish by inserting a swirled sweatband.

Trimming

❧ Add a self-fabric bow (page 110) and/or a rosette (page 111).

❧ Attach a veil for added drama and mystery.

❧ Sew on pearls, rhinestones, or artificial flowers.

❧ Add a feather trim (page 122).

❧ Add a "horsehair" brim (page 112).

THE GARLAND

A GARLAND IS A WREATH OF FLOWERS. PERHAPS THE MOST IMPORTANT ELEMENT IN GARLAND DESIGN IS THE COLOR HARMONY CREATED BY THE RIGHT CHOICE OF FLOWERS. GARDENING AND FLOWER-ARRANGING BOOKS MAKE GOOD SOURCES OF INSPIRATION, AS WELL AS YOUR NEIGHBORHOOD FLORIST SHOP.

MATERIALS

Artificial flowers (nice assortment of large and small ones with foliage; daisies, violets, and miniature roses make good choices)

#19 wire, twice the length of the headsize plus 3 inches (7.5 cm) for overlap

Tie wire

Strips of 1-inch-wide (2.5 cm) veiling material or No. 1 satin ribbon for wrapping the wire, about 3 yards (2.7 m) long

CONSTRUCTION

- ❧ Prepare the flowers and leaves by trimming the stems to 2 to 3 inches (5 to 7.5 cm) in length.
- ❧ Loop the wire to twice the size of the headsize and secure the overlap with tie wire. (See Figure 244.)
- ❧ Wrap the end of the veiling strip or ribbon around the wire at the center back. Secure the end with a few stitches.
- ❧ Place the first flower against the hoop and join the stem and the hoop by tightly wrapping them together with the veiling strip. Note: Do not try to work with a ribbon that is too long; it can get tangled with the flowers, thus disturbing the arrangement as well as slowing you down.
- ❧ Add a second flower and wrap again. (See Figure 245.)
- ❧ Continue on, mixing leaves and flowers, until the hoop is completely covered.
- ❧ Carefully grip the center front and center back and pull them in opposite directions to create an oval shape that fits your head well.

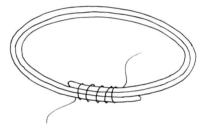

Figure 244

Figure 245

～ *Design Variations* ～

Tie small ribbon bows among the flowers; tie long satin ribbon streamers to the back of the garland and lightly swirl, weaving a swirl with the blunt edge of a knife; or make a semi-garland over a plastic head band, using the same technique.

TRIMMINGS

TRIMMING A HAT

A TRIM CAN TRANSFORM THE TOTAL LOOK OF A HAT. TRIMS CAN BE MADE FROM ALMOST ANYTHING—RIBBON, FELT SCRAPS, BEADS, FABRIC, LEATHER, FEATHERS, ARTIFICIAL FLOWERS. AS YOU BECOME MORE EXPERIENCED IN MILLINERY WORK, YOU WILL BE ABLE TO DRAW ON A LARGER VOCABULARY OF TRIMMINGS.

THE MOST IMPORTANT ASPECT OF HAT TRIMMING IS NOT WHAT YOU USE BUT HOW YOU APPLY IT. YOU MUST USE A LIGHT HAND. THE TRIM, WHETHER A BOW OR FLOWERS, SHOULD LOOK AS IF IT WERE BLOWN ONTO THE HAT AND IS NOW JUST RESTING THERE, LOOKING NATURAL.

ONE WAY TO ACHIEVE THIS LOOK IS TO TACK THE TRIM TO THE HAT INVISIBLY AND SECURELY WHILE AVOIDING TIGHT STITCHES. AFTER YOU HAVE PINNED THE TRIM TO THE HAT, ALL YOU NEED ARE A FEW LOOSE TIE STITCHES IN SEVERAL STRATEGIC PLACES. THE NUMBER OF TIES SHOULD BE PROPORTIONAL TO THE SIZE AND WEIGHT OF THE TRIM. DO NOT OVERDO IT OR THE HAT WILL LOOK TIGHT, ARTIFICIAL, AND 'HOMEMADE,' AS OPPOSED TO PROFESSIONAL.

RIBBONS AND BOWS

When you think about trimming a hat, the first images that come to mind are probably ribbons and bows. Used alone or combined, they provide quick, easy, and attractive adornments to any hat. The few examples that follow should give you a good starting point.

Figure 246

Ribbon As a Hatband Trim Around the Crown

- Swirl the ribbon, then pin it onto the starting point of the trim. It can be on the back, the front, or the side.
- Using the same color thread as your ribbon, tack the ribbon down at front, back, and sides. (You should tack the bottom of the ribbon—the edge that is closest to the brim.) Stick the needle through the loops on the edge of the ribbon as you stitch. Only a few stitches are needed to hold the trim in place. This can be done only with millinery ribbon, which has a saw-tooth edge that also gives the ribbon the elasticity needed for proper fit. Conceal the point where the ends meet with a tailored bow.

Figure 247

Tailored Bow

- Fold the ribbon into a loop and stitch ends together. (See Figure 246.)
- Cover the center with a matching piece of ribbon and stitch at the back. (See Figure 247.) This bow is flat and traditionally used on hatbands. (See Figure 248.)

Figure 248

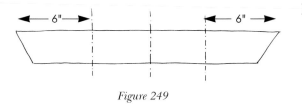

Fabric Bow

- ❧ Measure and cut a 10-inch-wide x 20-inch-long (25 x 50 cm) bias strip of fabric. Fold it lengthwise in half and cut the ends at a 45-degree angle.
- ❧ Stitch close to the edge all around, leaving a 1½-inch (4 cm) opening in the center.
- ❧ Turn the strip inside out through the opening, then stitch it closed with an invisible stitch.
- ❧ Mark the center of the band 6 inches (15 cm) in from each end side. (See Figure 249.)
- ❧ Bring each of the side marks to the center point of the band and fold the ribbon back out over itself. (See Figure 250.)
- ❧ Stitch the section where both folds meet.
- ❧ Pinch along the center and secure with a stitch. (See Figure 251.)
- ❧ You can also cover the center with a small strip of fabric as shown. (See Figure 252.)

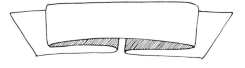

Figure 250

S ~ Bow

Measure and cut a 15-inch (38 cm) length of ribbon. Trim the ends at 45-degree angles. (See Figure 253.)

- ❧ Lay the ribbon on a flat surface in an S shape. (See Figure 254.)
- ❧ Carefully pinch together the center of the figure through all layers. (See Figure 255.)
- ❧ Secure the center with a strong stitch or a small strip of ribbon as shown before. (See Figure 256.)

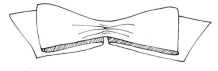

Figure 251

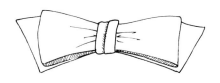

Figure 252

Figure 253

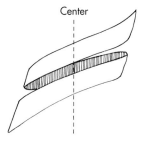

Figure 254

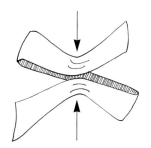

Figure 255

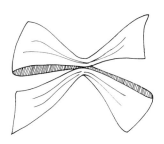

Figure 256

ROSETTES

Rosettes are easily made from a bias strip of fabric and add style to any hat. Use them in clusters of small and big ones and play with colors and pattern.

MATERIALS ———

Bias strip cut from a pretty fabric, about 4 inches (10 cm) wide and 12 inches (30 cm) long (Longer strips yield larger flowers.)

Needle and strong, color-matched thread

CONSTRUCTION ———

- Fold the strip in half lengthwise and trim the ends along the dotted line as shown. (See Figure 257.)
- With needle and strong thread, whip-stitch the edge from one sharp corner of the strip all the way to the other sharp one. (See Figure 258.)
- Remove the needle from the thread. Re-thread the needle with fresh thread and knot its end.
- Pull the loose thread so that the far corner starts curling upon itself. (See Figure 259.) This is the center of the flower. Secure the roll with a stitch or two at its base.
- Continue to shirr the strip by pulling the original thread. The strip will spiral around the center. Every turn around the center should be slightly larger, as in a real flower. (See Figure 260.)
- Keep securing the growing "petal" with stitches. As you work, make sure the base remains as flat as possible. (The flatter the base, the easier it attaches to the hat.)
- When you reach the end of the strip, take the corner and tuck it at the bottom of the flower. Secure with a final stitch.
- Use the rosette as is or mist with spray sizing to add stiffness.

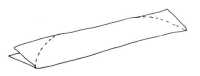

Figure 257

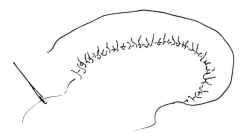

Figure 258

Figure 259

Figure 260

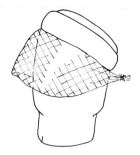

Figure 261

Figure 262

VEILS

The right veil can add a whole new dimension to a hat. The feminine and romantic heroines in old black-and-white movies often hid their beautiful eyes behind delicate and lacy mesh. Today, it is hard to find such variety of veil materials and styles. Yet you can liven up the basic color assortments of commercial veiling material by gluing on sequins, rhinestones, or tiny bows. Commercial veil material comes in 9- to 18-inch (23 - 46 cm) widths, enough to cover the eyes area or entire face.

MATERIALS

1 yard (.9 m) veiling strip

Thread in matching color

Straight pins

CONSTRUCTION

- ❧ Place the hat on the balsa headblock.
- ❧ Pin the center of the veiling strip at the center front of the hat.
- ❧ Drape the veil until you are pleased with the look, and then pin in place.
- ❧ Gather the cut ends of the veiling and wrap the thread around each end. (See Figure 261.)
- ❧ Tuck the ends under the edge of the crown and secure with a strong stitch.
- ❧ Stitch the veil to the crown by carefully catching the edge with needle and thread. (See Figure 262.)

HORSEHAIR BRIMS

Horsehair braid is no longer made of real horsehair, of course, but of nylon. It comes in many colors and widths, and is great for trimming and even whole hats. The following example will show you how to make a horsehair brim for the cocktail hat on page 102.

MATERIALS

1 yard (.9 m) of horsehair braid, 5 inches (13 cm) wide

Strong thread in matching color

Straight pins

Cocktail cap

CONSTRUCTION FOR A SHIRRED BRIM

- Note that one edge of the braid has a thread running through it. Find its end and very carefully start pulling and shirring the braid. The braid will begin to curl around itself like a snail. Do not pull too tight or too fast, otherwise you will break the thread.

Figure 263

- When about half of the braid is curled (about a 6-inch, 15 cm, length of pulled thread), fold the braid end lengthwise onto itself, bringing the unshirred corner to the shirred one. (See Figure 263.) Wrap the pulling thread tightly around it and secure with a knot. (See Figure 264.)

- Pin the knotted end to the center back of the cap. Line up the shirred edge of the braid with the edge of the cap. Start shirring the other end of the braid in the same manner.

Figure 264

- All the while, adjust the amount and degree of shirring to the shape of the cocktail cap, making it tighter at sharp angles and looser at wide ones.

- When done, fold the cut edge as described before and wrap the excess thread around the cut end. (See Figure 265.)

- Place both wrapped ends at the center back and secure with a few stitches. (See Figure 266.)

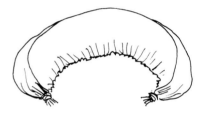

Figure 265

- Stitch the shirred edge to the edge of the cap.

- Insert the sweatband last, covering all raw edge of the brim.

CONSTRUCTION FOR A FLAT BRIM

- Shirr the horsehair braid as in the former example, but do not fold and wrap the raw ends. Instead, overlap them for 1 inch (2.5 cm) at the center back of the cap.

- Secure with a stitch and cover the raw edge with #3 millinery ribbon in a matching color or with a strip of pretty lace.

- Finish off in the same manner as for the shirred brim.

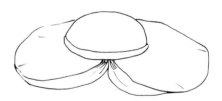

Figure 266

FINISHING TOUCHES

- Test the iron temperature on a scrap of horsehair. (Too high a setting will melt the material.) Carefully press the brim on a steam setting to remove excess surface wrinkles, working swiftly and purposefully.

- If desired, cover the center back where the brim ends meet with self-fabric flowers or a bow. (See Figure 267.) For a dressier look, glue on several rhinestones.

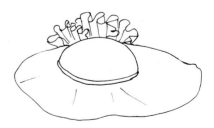

Figure 267

DYEING SILK FLOWERS

When you need to match a hat's trim color to a specific garment, it's easier to tint white silk flowers yourself than to shop for an exact color. To preserve the fresh appearance and shape of the flower, you should use a solvent-based tinting method.

First, though, a word of **caution**: Solvents are extremely flammable and dangerous if inhaled. Always work in a well-ventilated area, away from flame sources, and be sure to dispose of the solvent according to the instructions on the bottle or can. Do not pour solvent in the sink.

MATERIALS

Small tube of artist's oil paint (available at art-supply stores in endless colors and brands)

Artist's liquid thinner

Glass jar, large enough to fit the flower

Metal or wooden stirring stick

CONSTRUCTION

- Fill the glass jar with enough liquid thinner to cover the flower
- Mix in a very small amount of paint, It is best to start with a weak color solution and add more paint if you want a brighter color.
- Dip the flower in the solution for a couple of minutes. Remove it, carefully shaking off excess liquid, and let dry.
- The flower will dry very quickly as the thinner evaporates into the air. (Did you remember to open a window?)
- If you want a more intense color, add more paint to the jar, mix well, and repeat the process.
- When the flower is dry, you can add darker details to the petals and center, using a small brush dipped in a more concentrated form of the paint solution.

FEATHER TRIMS

Feathers make a wonderful trim material, adding personality and style to any hat. See pages 122–124 for a variety of trim options and information about purchasing and working with feathers.

FEATHERS

FEATHERS

Throughout the ages and among all cultures, feathers were used to adorn military helmets and hats, costumes, and jewelry. In the latter part of the 19th century, fashion dictated the use of entire birds on ladies' hats. Encouraged by market demand, a whole plume industry grew, causing the annihilation of many species around the world.

In 1896 the Audubon Society was founded to prevent the killing and extinction of these rare birds as associated with the plume trade. Many species, including the bird of paradise and the egret, are protected by laws in practically every state. Using and possessing rare, imported feathers is illegal, but there are many imitations that look just like the real thing. The feathers listed here, used alone or in combination, are both beautiful and legal.

Ostrich (plume, burnt), turkey (quills and wings), pheasant (colorful male and muted colors female), peacock (golden, blue-tip, tail, strung herl), goose (short and medium plumage), rooster (coq or cock), marabou (turkey's down), Guinea hen (gray feathers with white specks), duck (domestic and wild).

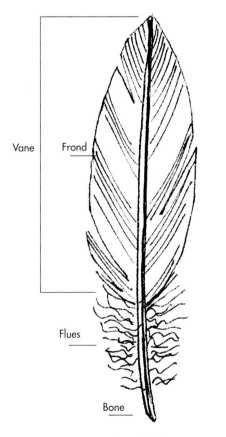

Figure 268

MILLINERY FEATHERS

Anatomy of a Millinery Feather

The **bone** or stem is the horny/bony spine portion of a feather. It is grooved on the front and smooth at the back. The **vane** is the flattened, hairlike part of feather. The **fronds** are the many parallel, hairlike filaments that make up the vane. **Flues** or fluff is the fuzzy, woolly portion at the base of the feather. (See Figure 268.)

Commercial Categories of Feathers

Feathers are available in various forms, some of which are listed below.

Pads ～ Individual feathers are glued to felt pads that are used when large areas need to be covered quicker and at a relatively lower cost than with feathers applied singly. Pads are available in many bright colors as well as in special patterns and textures. When buying pads, make sure that the feathers are firmly affixed and that the glue is not dried out and crumbling.

Strung ～ After feathers are selected for quality and size, they are strung together into a long strip of feathers of same color, quality, and length, all facing one direction. Do not confuse strung feathers with boas!!

Decorative Boas ～ Boas are long, fluffy scarves made of feathers in varying lengths of one or mixed bird feathers. All the feathers are full and fluffy in all directions. Use boas as a trim around the brim of a hat or for sectional trims, such as fluffy pompons on the side of a close-fitting cap. Boas are not a suitable source for hats covered with individual feathers.

Loose -· These feathers are sold by weight and are available as selected and not-selected feathers. They are used primarily for trimming.

Skins -· These feathers come attached to a whole bird's skin. The most widespread type of skin feathers come from ring-necked pheasants, which are naturally very colorful and provide a wide array of colors and sizes.

Feather suppliers sell their feathers by weight, with the exception of boas, which are sold by length. In general, millinery-supply sources will carry feathers for trimming only. If you are looking for quality and variety, buy your feathers from a dealer who specializes in them.

Commercial Terminology of Feathers

The feather trade has developed its own terminology to describe feathers; here are a few examples. (See pages 38 and 39 for four-color examples.)

Plumage -· Collective name for small feathers from the neck and chest areas of birds.

Plume -· A large, ornamental feather, commonly of an ostrich.

"Schlappen" -· Rooster feathers off the tail section. Small, skinny, and pointed, they are available in strung and boa forms.

Chandelle -· Turkey flat feathers (from the bottom back section of the turkey) are stripped and sliced lengthwise along the bone and made into boas.

Flues -· The fuzzy-woolly fluff portion at the base of the bone.

Hackle -· Rooster feathers. Saddle hackle are long, slender, and pointy. Neck hackle are long and slender with a rounder, fuller base.

Cosse -· Short, stiff feathers of any bird.

Herl -· Peacock feathers that can be acid-burned to remove the fronds. The burnt herl looks like delicate, stiff thread; bundled, it is used for trimming.

Nagoires (pronounced nay-jo-res) -· Shoulder feathers of goose. They make a good choice for covering a hat with individual feathers.

Parried Feathers ~ The bone (stem) was ground down to make the feather pliable and easy to shape. May be used for both covering and trimming.

Quill ~ Stiff, long feather from the wing.

Biot (pronounced bee-oh) ~ Stiff, short feathers made by stripping the vane part off the bone as a single unit. The result looks like a long strip of fake eyelashes. Twist the strip around wire to make whisklike brush trimmings, or make bristly pompons.

DYEING FEATHERS

Feathers can be purchased raw (natural), degraded (bleached), or dyed. Brightly colored feathers are first bleached, then dyed. Darker, more muted shades, such as dark burgundy, or green, are the result of dyeing raw feathers. Dyeing is cost effective only if you require a commercially large number of feathers in a custom- matched color. The feathers are dyed in big vats similar to the process used for dyeing textiles. Your feather dealer will be able to provide cost and quantity details upon request.

STORING FEATHERS

Moths love raw feathers!! Dyed feathers, however, will not be bothered by moths. Store your raw feathers in a tightly sealed container with a few mothballs. When ready to use, just steam and fluff the feathers.

Straight-blade Knife

HANDLING FEATHERS

Feathers are quite durable and with proper care will last for many years. Before using feathers, steam them to restore their fluff and sheen. This is true for raw feathers as well as ones already affixed to hats. The natural oil on your skin can improve the look of a dull feather; stroke it between your thumb and forefinger a few times. Manipulating feathers requires two special tools: a straight-blade knife for cutting and a curved-blade knife for curling.

Curved-blade Knife

DESIGNING WITH FEATHERS

There are numerous techniques that will transform any ordinary bunch of feathers into an unusual trim. Several of these techniques are explained in the pages that follow. I encourage you to look at paintings and drawings of costumes throughout history. Many of these depict society women and military officers wearing the loveliest feather creations, and they make good sources of inspiration.

FEATHER-PADS COVERED HAT

F EATHER PADS ALLOW YOU TO COMPLETE A FEATHER HAT IN A RELATIVE-
LY SHORT TIME. WHILE COVERING AN ENTIRE HAT WITH PADS IS A PER-
FECTLY ACCEPTABLE PRACTICE, YOU CAN ACHIEVE MORE INTERESTING AND
UNUSUAL RESULTS IF YOU COMBINE THIS METHOD WITH PLACING THE FEATH-
ERS ON SINGLY AS SHOWN IN THE ONE-BY-ONE FEATHERS HAT THAT FOLLOWS.

MATERIALS

Foundation frame in a simple shape
(blocked wool felt or blocked
buckram covered with flalean)

White adhesive (I prefer Sobo)

Paring knife or small spatula (for
applying the glue)

Feather pads (one dozen will cover
an average crown)

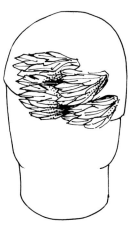

Steam

Figure 269

CONSTRUCTION

- Start by steaming the pads with directed steam jets from a
  steam iron to help the feathers regain their natural curl so
  they will better conform to the rounded shape of the crown.
  Lightly assist the process with your fingers, working first on
  the wrong side of the pad and then the right side. (See
  Figure 269.)

- To best determine the proper placement of the pads on the
  crown, do a "dry" test. Pin the pads on the crown, arranging
  the pads from the bottom of the crown up and overlapping
  slightly to prevent the raw base from showing. The feathers
  should form an uninterrupted flow. If your design includes
  feathers extending below the edge of the crown (in brimless
  hats), no pad base should be visible on the inside. (See
  Figure 270.)

- Mix the adhesive well to an even consistency. Remove the pads
  from the foundation frame and apply a thin layer of adhesive
  to the part of the hat you'll be covering and a matching
  adhesive layer to the pad section. Take care not to get adhesive
  on the feathers! Press the pad to the crown, then repeat the
  process until the crown is completely covered. Most important,
  remember to overlap the pads so their base will not be visible.

- Let dry completely, then use a few jets of steam from a steam
  iron to add finishing styling touches.

Figure 270

~ Design Hints ~

Glue in single feathers to fill in
gaps or add contrasting color; add
a complementing feather trim.

ONE-BY-ONE FEATHER HAT

THE SECRET TO COVERING A SURFACE WITH A SMOOTH, UNBROKEN FLOW OF FEATHERS LIES IN A SPECIAL TECHNIQUE OF GLUING THEM DOWN ONE BY ONE. EACH NEW FEATHER COVERS THE RAW BASE OF THE PREVIOUS FEATHER. THE POSSIBILITIES ARE STAGGERING…IMAGINE FANTASY HATS? HOW ABOUT DUPLICATING AN ENTIRE BIRD ON A HAT? (PHEASANTS ARE GREAT FOR THIS PURPOSE.)

MATERIALS

Good quality strung feathers (best beginner's choice are 3- to 4-inch-long, 7.5 to 10 cm, turkey flats or goose nagoires)

Feather knife (straight blade)

Wool felt hat with simple round crown (use an old one for practice)

Large steamer tray with mesh bottom

Rubber cement adhesive in an airtight container

Small, shallow glass cup

Long strip of paper, 1 inch (2.5 cm) wide

Steamer

Twist

Figure 271

Figure 272

Figure 273

Note: The following instructions may seem uncomplicated, but making good feather hats in this method is a very challenging process, requiring patience, attention to detail, and lots of practice.

CONSTRUCTION

❧ Place the strung feathers in the mesh tray and steam them for two to three minutes until they are fluffy. From time to time, grab them by the strung portion and shake them in the air as if they were covered with dust. DO NOT GET THE FEATHERS WET!

❧ Pull or cut each feather off of the connecting string.

❧ Look through your feathers and discard any that are torn or have sections missing. If a feather is split but otherwise intact, place it between your thumb and middle finger and 'comb' it with your fingertips until the gap closes. Save the nicest feathers for the top of the crown since it is the first spot people see in a finished hat.

❧ Use the knife to trim off the base of each feather, leaving ½-inch (13 mm) flues on. Successful cutting actions come from the wrist: Place the straight edge of the knife against the bone and twist the wrist up and out. (See Figure 271.)

- Pour a small amount of adhesive into the glass cup. This adhesive is volatile and dries fast, so work quickly and precisely. Use the knife to spread some adhesive on center top of the crown.

- Dip only the flues of each feather in adhesive and arrange them on the center top as shown in the following sequence. (See Figures 272, 273, 274, and 275.) The flues form a pillow that elevates the next feather head so it doesn't look plastered down, but instead has dimension and character. Rest each successive feather's head over the flues.

- When the top section starts sloping to the side, it is time to place a 'lift' at center back.

CREATING THE 'LIFT'

- Fold the paper strip in half lengthwise and pin it along the center back as a 'lift.' (See Figure 276.) Do not remove the 'lift' until you have completed gluing on the very last feather!!

- Glue the feathers in a form of overlapping columns (not spiraling circles!), starting the first column at center back, and work clockwise. (See Figure 277.) The feather buildup should be deliberate and careful. Aim for variety but maintain the direction and flow of the feathers. (See Figure 278.)

- When the last column reaches the 'lift,' glue on one more column, slipping the flues under the 'lift' and feather heads of the first column. (See Figures 279 and 280.)

- Remove the lift. The seam should be invisible.

FINISHING

- Add some styling to the feathers with a few shots of steam from a steam iron. Pull out any visible 'cowlicks.'

- With clean fingers, stroke the feathers in their natural growing direction to smooth out any parted sections. (The feathers are quite durable.)

- Store the completed hat away from dust and direct sunlight. If you have used raw feathers (not dyed), store in a closed hat box with a moth-repellant.

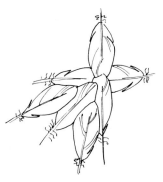

Figure 274

Figure 275

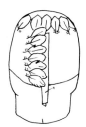

Figure 276

Figure 277

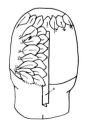

Figure 278

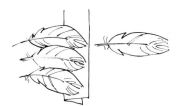

Figure 279

Figure 280

FEATHER TRIMMING

FEATHER TRIMS ADD EXCITEMENT AND STYLE TO ANY HEAD WEAR. FOLLOWING ARE JUST A FEW OF MANY WAYS TO CREATE TRIMS FROM FEATHERS.

PLUMAGE ROSE WITH CENTER COQ FEATHERS

MATERIALS

> 5 coq feathers, each 5 inches (13 cm) long
>
> 3-inch-long (7.5 cm) strip of strung 3-inch turkey plumage
>
> Tie wire

CONSTRUCTION

- ❧ Steam the feathers to regain fluff and sheen.
- ❧ Hold all five coq feathers in one hand and tightly wrap tie wire around their base.
- ❧ Wrap the strung plumage around the coq feathers and secure with tie wire.

PLUMAGE ROSE WITH STRIPPED COQ FEATHERS AND BURNT PEACOCK HERL CENTER

Figure 281

MATERIALS

> 5 coq feathers, each 8 inches (20 cm) long
>
> Small bundle of burnt peacock herl
>
> 3-inch-long (7.5 cm) strip of strung 3-inch turkey plumage, optional
>
> Tie wire
>
> Feather knife (straight)

CONSTRUCTION

- ❧ Steam the feathers to regain fluff and sheen.
- ❧ Strip the coq feathers by holding a feather in your left hand and a feather knife in your other hand. (See Figures 281 and 282.) Leaving about 1½ inches (4 cm) from the top, start stripping the fronds in a peeling motion to create a delicate-looking stem with a full pointed tip.

Figure 282

- Bundle the stripped feathers together with the herl. Secure the bundle with tie wire at the base.
- Wrap strung turkey plumage around the bundle to create a "rose" as in the previous trim.

BOA POMPON

MATERIALS

Boa of chandelle or other dense feathers such as goose or turkey (Boas are sold by length. Buy the shortest one you can find and use what's left over to trim other hats.)

Tie wire

CONSTRUCTION

- Steam the feathers to regain fluff and sheen.
- Cut off the last 2 inches (5 cm) from the boa's pointed end.
- Hold the blunt end of the section and smooth the feathers with your hand as if you were making a pony tail.
- Wrap the exposed blunt end with tie wire and steam again to fluff.

CURLED TAIL FEATHER

MATERIALS

A long feather (e.g., long ostrich plume or pheasant tail feather)

Feather knife (curling)

CONSTRUCTION

The idea here is to create a deep bend in the bone of the feather. You may wish to practice this technique on coq feathers before trying it on the more expensive tail feathers.

- Hold the feather in your left hand and the knife in your right hand. The feather has a slight natural curl so all you do is emphasize the curl so the feather coils upon itself. The smooth side of the 'bone' is considered the front and the grooved side is the back.
- Gently "break" the back of the bone in ½-inch (13 mm) intervals, working from the tip to the base. Be careful not to crack the front or the "bone" will really break.
- Steam the feather to regain fluff and sheen.
- Attach the coiled feather so that it encircles a crown or perches on a cocktail hat. The feather can also be used as a hair ornament by itself, perhaps with a bow at the base.

COQ-TAIL COCKTAIL

MATERIALS ────────────

4 black coque tail feathers, 12 - 14
   inches (31 - 36 cm) long

3 schlappen feathers in a natural color,
   3 - 4 inches long (7.5 - 10 cm)

2 dyed-red schlappen feathers,
   2 inches (5 cm) long

1 dyed-yellow guinea hen feather
   in yellow, 1 inch (2.5 cm) long

Tie wire

Color-matched florist tape or strip
   of veiling

CONSTRUCTION ────────────

* Steam the feathers to regain fluff and sheen.
* Layer the feathers so the shortest one lies on top.
* Wrap the exposed end with tie wire and steam to fluff.
* Conceal the wire with color-matched florist tape or with a strip
  of veiling.

BEYOND BASICS

THE MILLINERY WORKROOM

İT IS DIFFICULT TO SUGGEST MORE THAN GENERAL GUIDELINES FOR THE LAYOUT OF A MILLINERY WORKROOM. MAKING CUSTOM HATS IS INTIMATE AND PERSONAL WORK. THE WORKROOM PROJECTS BOTH THE PERSONAL STYLE OF THE USER AND THE PHYSICAL LIMITATIONS OF THE SPACE. MILLINERY IS LEARNED BY DOING. AS YOU BECOME MORE EXPERIENCED, YOUR WORK AREA, TOO, WILL GO THROUGH MANY CHANGES.

A TYPICAL WORK SPACE IS DIVIDED IN TWO MAIN AREAS: CONSTRUCTION AND FINISHING. THE CONSTRUCTION AREA CONTAINS THE EQUIPMENT NECESSARY FOR PATTERN DEVELOPMENT, SEWING, AND STEAMING. THE FINISHING AREA IS WHERE THE HATS ARE TRIMMED AND FINISHED. KEEP THIS DIVISION FLEXIBLE FOR OCCASIONAL CHANGES IN WORK STYLE. WHATEVER THE LAYOUT, DO DEVELOP A SYSTEM FOR KEEPING TRACK OF EQUIPMENT AND TOOLS. NOTHING IS MORE FRUSTRATING AND TIME CONSUMING THAN LOOKING FOR RIBBON OR A CERTAIN THREAD COLOR THAT YOU JUST KNOW IS THERE BUT CANNOT LOCATE WHEN YOU MOST NEED IT.

MANY OF THE TOOLS USED IN MILLINERY WORK ARE READILY AVAILABLE IN HARDWARE STORES OR IN SEWING SUPPLY STORES AND MAIL ORDER CATALOGS. MOST WOULD BE FAMILIAR TO ANYONE WITH EVEN SLIGHT SEWING EXPERIENCE. OTHER TOOLS ARE SPECIFIC TO THE MILLINERY TRADE AND CAN ONLY BE FOUND AT SPECIALIZED SUPPLY SOURCES.

MILLINERY SUPPLIES SUCH AS FELT, STRAW, AND BUCKRAM ARE ALSO SUBJECT TO SUPPLY AND DEMAND IN THE INDUSTRY. FROM TIME TO TIME THESE MATERIALS MAY BECOME SCARCE, UNAVAILABLE, OR AVAILABLE ONLY IN VERY LARGE QUANTITIES. IMPROVISE! HATS CAN BE MADE FROM A VARIETY OF NATURAL AND MANMADE MATERIALS. SUBSTITUTE AN UNAVAILABLE ITEM WITH ONE THAT PRODUCES A SIMILAR EFFECT UNTIL SUPPLY IS REPLENISHED.

BASICS FOR A MILLINERY WORKROOM

Good lighting

Large work surface

Basic sewing notions

A few yards of foundation materials (buckram, flexie, French elastic, flalean, muslin)

Assorted fashion fabrics (velvet, tweed, jersey, silks, lace, brocade, wools)

Bridal satin in several colors for lining

Millinery ribbons in various sizes and colors for sweatbands and trims

Balsa headsize blocks in several sizes

Portable steamer (For best results, invest in a quality brand.)

Sewing machine with free arm

Tissue paper for stuffing finished hats

Hat boxes

Large mirror and a hand mirror

Index cards listing regular customers, their preferences, colors, head size, etc.

Labels

Business cards

STARTING A SMALL MILLINERY BUSINESS

THE ORDERS ARE FLOWING IN, YOUR BUSINESS IS GROWING, AND IT'S TIME TO MOVE OUT OF THE KITCHEN INTO A COMMERCIAL SPACE. THERE'S A LOT MORE TO STARTING A BUSINESS THAN JUST SIGNING A LEASE, THOUGH. PLEASE READ ON. THE PROCESSES MAY VARY FROM STATE TO STATE.

Name

Choose a name for your business. It could be your name or some catchy, fictitious name such as 'Happy Hats.' Check industry directories and the phone book to make sure that no other business has the same name.

If you use a name other than your own, you will need to have it registered as 'fictitious business name' with the county clerk. It is also called D.B.A. (doing business as) notice and will be useful when opening a commercial bank account. Call the local county clerk's office for exact requirements.

Commercial Bank Account

Keep your personal finances separate from your business finances. Open a commercial bank account and establish a line of credit.

Licenses

Contact your local Division of Permits and Licenses. Ask if you need a license for your type of business and request an information pack.

Resale Number

Apply for a Certificate of Authority at your local business tax office. Having a resale number exempts you from paying tax on hatmaking supplies.

IRS

Apply for a federal employer ID number for filing federal tax statements.

Renting Commercial Space

Register for applicable business taxes at your local City Collector's office.

Invoices

Purchase a generic invoice book or print one with your company's name and address on it. This will not only help you keep track of your transactions, but is also required by law.

Bookkeeping

Tidy bookkeeping will make filing your tax statements an easy task. You can do it manually or on a computer with one of the many accounting software packages that generate invoices, write checks, and plan budgets. Either way, enrolling in an accounting course or small business management course at your local community college is highly recommended.

With all the paperwork in place, you should know a few things about what guides the millinery industry. Several times a year manufacturers show their creations at trade shows across the country. Store buyers select the styles they like and place their orders. These shows follow a predictable pattern.

- The spring line is prepared in October, shown in November, and sold from December through March.

- The Resort & Holiday line is prepared in June, shown in August, reaches stores in November/December, and is sold through February.

- The fall line 1 is prepared in January, shown in March/April, reaches stores in May/June, and is sold through October.

- The fall line 2 is prepared in February, shown in late April/May, reaches stores from July through October, and is sold through December.

The New York market weeks, for example, are typically:

Summer: January 5-12

Fall 1: March 2-6

Fall 2: March 30 - April 6

Resort: August 3-10

Spring: October 26 - November 2

Even if you do not participate in these shows, the above dates will give you an indication of when to approach store buyers with your collection of seasonal hats.

PRICING A HAT

Whether you sell custom hats or fill wholesale orders, it is important to understand your target market and set your prices accordingly. Unfortunately, there are no set rules for pricing hats. One way is to compare your work to what is offered at stores, but keep in mind that the store usually adds at least 100% to a hat's wholesale price. A custom hat, of course, made especially to the headsize and other requirements of your customer, may command a higher price. In any case, make sure that your price covers the cost of materials as well as your time invested in making it.

A word about time. An inexperienced milliner will take longer than an experienced one to make a given hat. In other words, as you are learning a new hat style or technique, expect a smaller profit margin.

APPENDIX I

THE MILLINERY RULER

This unique and handy tool can be used to draw circles of any size. Simply mark the center of a sheet of pattern paper; insert a pushpin through a hole on the ruler to anchor it in the center; then insert the point of a sharp pencil into another hole, a measured distance away. As you swing the pencil around, it will draw a circular line on the paper.

To make such a ruler you need a transparent plastic ruler (available in any art-supply store), 18 inches long and 2 inches wide (46 cm x 5 cm). With a drill make holes in the plastic ruler as indicated below. To make the ruler even sturdier, you may want to glue a metal ruler (the same length but only ⅞ inch, 22 mm, wide) along the undrilled portion of the ruler. (See Figures 283 and 284.)

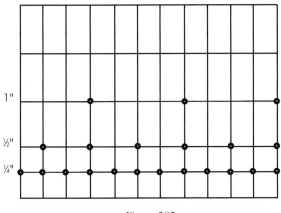

Figure 283

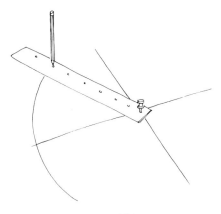

Figure 284

APPENDIX II

HEADSIZE PLATE ———————————————————————

Adjust to a larger or smaller headsize by using the 22-inch (56 cm) headsize pattern below as a starting point. (See Figure 285.)

For sizes larger than 22 inches add the following:
For size 22½ inches (57 cm) add ⅛ inch (3 mm) all around
For size 23 inches (59 cm) add ¼ inch (6 mm) all around
For size 23½ inches (60 cm) add ⅜ inch (9 mm) all around
For size 24 inches (61 cm) add ½ inch (13 mm) all around

For sizes smaller than 22 inches decrease by the following:
For size 21½ inches (55 cm) decrease by ⅛ inch all around
For size 21 inches (53 cm) decrease by ¼ inch all around
For size 20½ inches (52 cm) decrease by ⅜ inch all around
For size 20 inches (50 cm) decrease by ½ inch all around

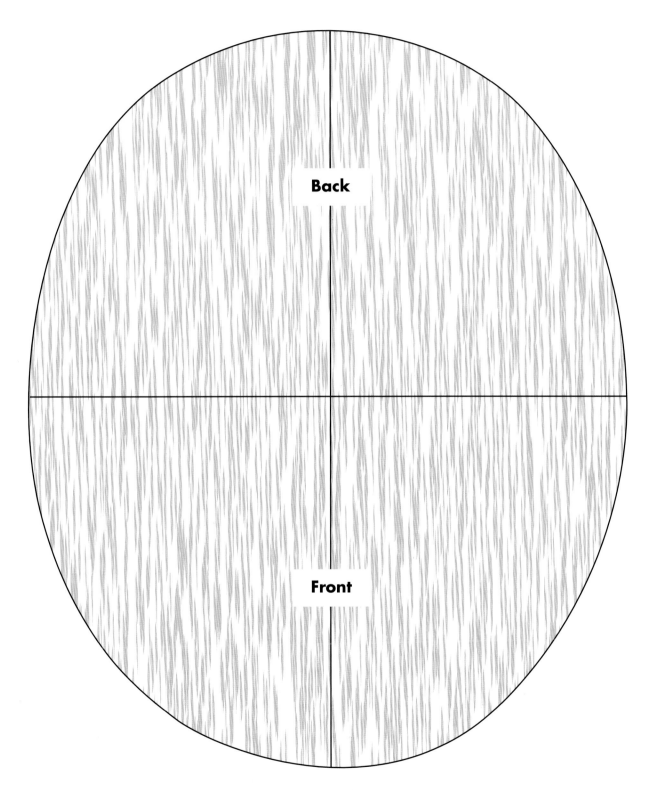

Back

Front

Figure 285

APPENDIX III

THE PRESSING ROLL

A pressing roll is used to support curved seams while pressing. To make a pressing roll, trace the pattern below on a pressing cloth, adding a ½-inch (13 mm) seam allowance. Stitch all around, leaving a small opening. Turn the case inside out, stuff it with cotton batting, and stitch the opening closed. To use the pressing roll, hold the pressing roll in one hand under the fabric and press the seam open with a steam iron. (See Figures 286 and 287.)

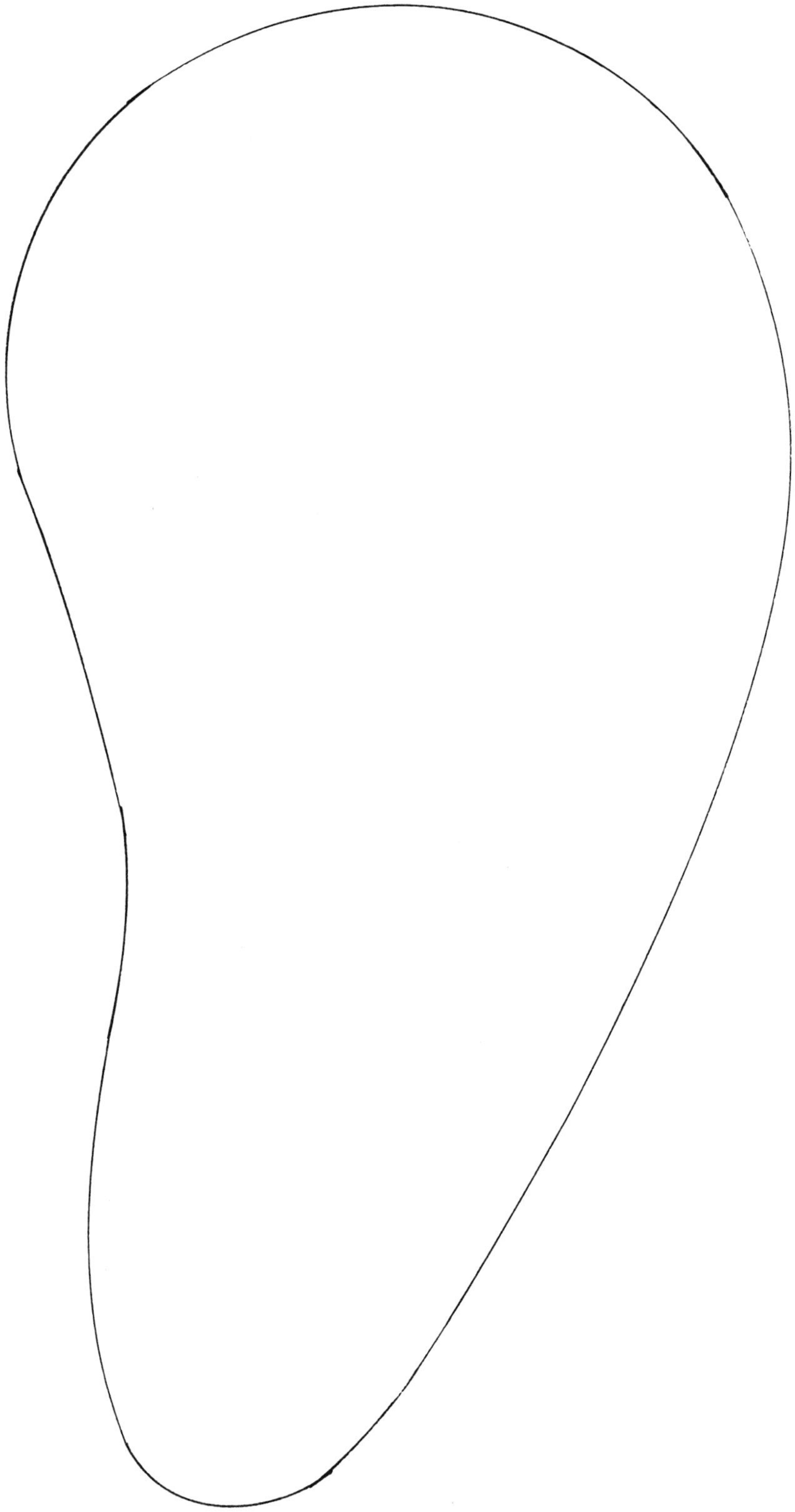

Figure 286

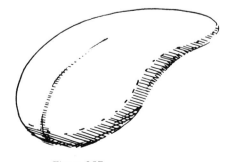

Figure 287

APPENDIX IV

THE MILLINERY FRENCH CURVE

A French curve like the one illustrated below is available only through millinery suppliers. (See Figure 288.)

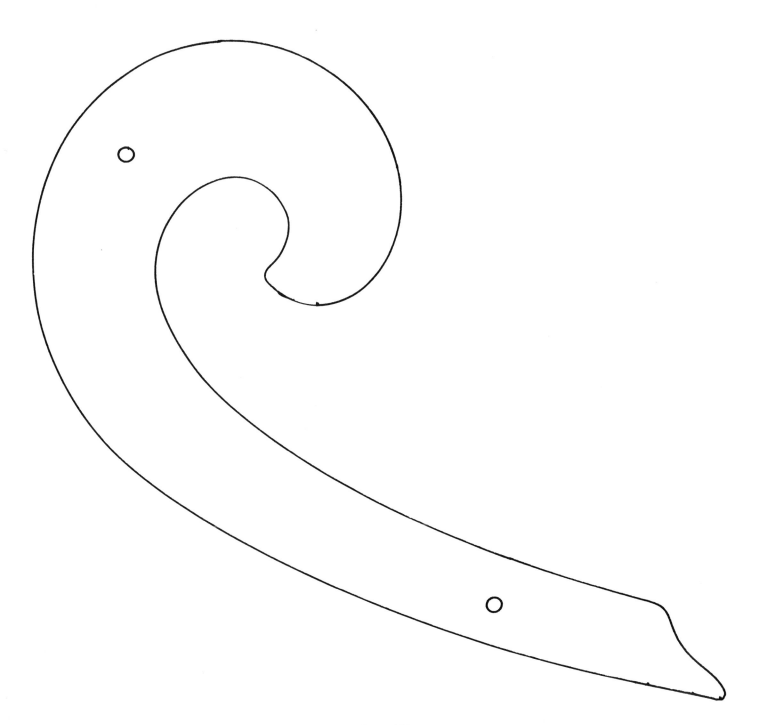

Figure 288

GLOSSARY

Agal A rolled band of decorative material used to secure the traditional Arab headdress.

Alpine or **Tyrolian** A soft, felt hat with a turned-up back brim, usually decorated with a feather, brush, or tassel.

Alibuntal A finely woven, smooth straw made from the stems of the Philippine buntal palm.

Baku Straw made from Ceylon palms.

Basting Stitch A temporary stitch used in millinery and dressmaking.

Beret A large, brimless cap with a flat crown of varying widths. Berets were commonly used during the Hellenic period and have been a perennial favorite ever since.

Bias (true bias) In woven fabrics, a direction 45 degrees off the straight grain.

Bias Binding A ready-made binding strip with the edges turned in.

Bias Cut Fabric cut on a bias so it can stretch in length as well as in width.

Bicorne (by-corn) A wide-brimmed hat with two upturned corners. This style was worn by Napoleon I and is also called Chapeau Bras.

Bird Cage A small hat with stiffened veiling surrounding the wearer's face.

Bird of Paradise Feathers An endangered bird with a long, soft, graceful plume.

Block A solid form in a shape of a hat, commonly made of wood (ash or balsa). Used to manipulate and shape millinery materials such as felt or straw into hats using steam and heat.

Blocking The act of hatmaking using a block.

Boater A flat-brimmed hat with a small crown, mostly made of straw coated with shellac. Sailors were fashionable in the late 19th century for sailing and general outdoor wear. Also called Sailor.

Bonnet A head covering that frames the face and is tied with a ribbon under the chin.

Bow Tied or sewn loops of ribbon; used as millinery trim.

Bowler A stiff hat with a medium, domed crown with an accentuated upward roll at the sides. In 19th-century England, bowlers were worn with formal riding attire and were popularized by the Earl of Derby.

Breton A hat with a round crown and a wide brim upturned evenly all around; originally part of the traditional peasant costume in Brittany, France.

Brim The part of the hat that flares out from the crown.

Brimmer A hat with a broad brim.

Buckram Heavily sized coarse cotton mesh used for making a stiff foundation for fabric-covered hats.

Bumper Brim A tubular brim found on several hat types.

Calotte or **Calot** A close-fitting skull cap.

Cape Net A stiffened cotton net used as a foundation in hat brims and crowns.

Cartwheel A hat with a large straight brim and a short crown. The style is reminiscent of the hats worn by peasants in southern France.

Casablanca A hat with a shallow crown and an inverted, downward sloping brim, popularized by the film Casablanca.

Casque Any close-fitting, helmetlike hat. The term is derived from the French word for helmet.

Cavalier Hat A large-brimmed, plumed hat worn with the brim pinned up on the right side so the wearer's sword arm could move freely through the air. This hat type was worn by cavaliers in mid-17th century.

Cellophane Woven straw braid made into hat bodies and bands.

Chenille Fabric of wool, cotton, silk, or rayon that has a tufted, velvetlike pile. Chenille is the French word for caterpillar.

Chiffon Sheer, woven fabric with a soft finish.

Ciré A patent leather finish on fabric, ribbon, or straw. The word means "polish" in French.

Cloche A close-fitting hat with a bell-shaped crown. Cloches were first popularized in the 1920s.

Cockade Pleated ribbon rosette used in trimming.

Coq Feathers Long, iridescent black or dark green feathers of a cock or rooster. Used in trimmings and boas.

Conch Hat A wide-brimmed straw hat worn in the Caribbean. The palm leaf edges are left unfinished.

Coolie Hat A one-piece, cone-shaped straw hat that slopes down from a peaked crown. It is similar to the hats worn by Chinese laborers.

Coalman Hat A short visor cap with a protective flap at the back, derived from the hats worn by English coal deliverers to protect their backs from dust.

Coonskin Cap A hat style originally worn by American frontier men, but also popular in the U.S. in the 1950s. It was made out of raccoon fur with the tail hanging down the back.

Corduroy Pile fabric woven with either a wide or narrow wale. It is formed by adding an extra filling row.

Crinoline A cheeseclothlike thin mesh, firmly sized.

Crown Section of the hat that covers the head.

Crown Tip The top part of the hat crown.

Cuff A brim that folds up against the outer side of the crown.

Deer Stalker A hunting cap with visors in the front and back, and ear flaps that tie up over the crown. It is also called the Sherlock Holmes hat.

Derby *See Bowler.*

Doll Hat A very small hat in any style. Originally made as part of a doll's costume, the term is applied generally to any whimsical miniature hat worn forward on the head.

Drape The way a fabric hangs or falls. In millinery work it is the term used to describe the way fabric folds cover a hat frame or block.

Egret (Heron) An endangered bird. Imitation egret feathers are made from goat hair and by acid burning the flues off of ostrich quills.

Elastic A tubular cord or flat band woven with rubber thread that allows it to stretch.

Fabric A loom-woven cloth. Fabric has two sides: the right or top side (which is intended for display) and the wrong side or the back of the material.

Fedora A low-crown, soft, felt hat with a lengthwise crease in the crown and a moderate brim, rolled slightly at the sides.

Felt A firm material made of matted fibers, wool, or animal fur by a process of interlocking the hairs or threads by twisting, rolling, moistening, and drying.

Fez A brimless felt cap that is conical and is trimmed with a tassel. This hat is the national headwear of Turks.

Feather Pads Small feathers arranged and pasted to a felt patch foundation.

Fish Tail Ribbon with a V-shape cut out at the end.

Flalean Material used as interlining in making soft hats. It has soft pile on one side and is smooth on the other (also spelled "flalene").

Flexible Buckram (flexie) Similar to buckram, this fabric is a coarse cotton mesh; it is unsized and very flexible. Used in hat foundations.

Flues The fuzzy fibers extending from each side of the stem (bone) of a feather or quill. They give the feather its full look.

French Elastic Fine cotton mesh used for light hat foundations.

Foundation Frame A shaped frame made of buckram or flexie and then covered with fashion fabric.

Fusing Agents Available in sheet or liquid form and used under heat to fuse two layers of fabric to each other.

Gainsborough A hat with a large brim turned up on one side and trimmed with a plume. The style was made fashionable through the paintings of 19th-century English painter Gainsborough.

Gaucho Hat A black hat with a shallow crown and wide flat brim, tied under the chin. It was adapted from hats worn by South American cowboys.

Gondolier's Hat A sailor hat with a slanted brim and shallow crown, decorated with a wide ribbon band and streamers. It is similar to those worn by Venetian gondoliers.

Grain The direction of the warp threads in woven fabrics. (See Warp.)

Grosgrain Ribbon with heavy crosswise ribs and a rounded cord finish to the edges.

Guinea Hen Feathers Gray feathers with white specks, used in pads and trimmings.

Hackle Long, slender feathers on the neck of the coq or rooster.

Haberdasher A dealer of men's hats, ties, shirts, and gloves.

Halo Hat A hat worn at the back of the head, creating a circular frame around the face.

Headblock A head-shaped form made of hardwood or balsa used to shape or reshape a hat. It is also called a crown or skull block. Headblocks are expressed by the headsize.

Headsize The circumference of the head (in inches or centimeters) just above the brows and ears.

Headsize Collar A rim or flange extending from the brim at a 90-degree angle.

Hennin A high, cone-shaped hat with a veil hanging down the side, worn by 15th- century women.

Homburg A man's felt hat with a soft, lengthwise dent in the crown and a shallow, slightly rolled brim.

Horsehair (*Crin* in French) A wide, woven braid once made of real horsehair, but nowadays made of synthetic filaments.

Interlining A layer of material placed between the fashion fabric and the lining.

Juliet Cap A small, brimless, round cap of wide mesh, mostly decorated with jewels. The style dates back to the Renaissance and today is popular in bridal wear.

Klaft The striped cloth headdress of Egyptian Pharaohs.

Leghorn Fine hat straw imported from Italy.

Lining Fabric such as taffeta which is used to cover the inside surface of a hat.

Maline A soft, thin, gauzy silk, cotton, or nylon similar to net in weave. It comes in 18-inch widths in many colors and is used for trimming (a.k.a. tulle or illusion).

Marabou An African stork with soft, white feathers on its tail and wings. Used in trimmings and boas.

Mercerized Cotton Thread Cotton thread treated with sodium hydroxide to add strength and luster, and make dyeing easier.

Milan A fine, closely woven straw braid originally made in Italy and used for machine- sewn hats.

Milliner's Needle A long sewing needle with a large eye used in millinery work; also called 'straws.'

Millinery Associated in the 16th century with the city of Milan (Italy), which was renowned for accessories, gloves, and trims. Later the term became synonymous with all feminine headgear.

Millinery Adhesive A colorless, water-based fabric adhesive.

Millinery Ribbon Sawtooth-edge ribbon made of a rayon/cotton blend. Also referred to as petersham, belting ribbon, or as picot in French.

Millinery Thread Strong glazed thread that doesn't snag or tangle easily.

Millinery Wires Wires used to reinforce hat frames or brims; the wires are covered with silk, rayon, or paper.

Mushroom Hat A hat with a mushroomlike, downward brim .

Nap A fabric finish that has been brushed to raise the surface.

Open Crown A hat with a complete brim and open top crown.

Overcast Stitch Used to prevent a fabric's raw edge from unraveling.

Panama A soft, handwoven straw hat with a medium brim and a rounded crown. Was first made of the Ecuadorian jipijapa plant.

Panamalaque A buntal-weave hat body made of visca fiber.

Panné Velvet A lustrous velvet with its pile pressed flat in one direction.

Paralaque A type of straw material with a lustrous finish.

Peacock Feathers The long tail feathers of the peacock are popular both dyed and in their natural colors. Acid burning gives the fronds a crisp appearance. Used in clusters for an aigrette effect.

Pheasant Feathers Used in their natural brilliant colors for best effect, either in the one-by-one method or in pads to cover a hat foundation. The long tail feathers are used as trims.

Picture Hat A very large brimmed hat trimmed with wide ribbon and a bow and worn tilted to the side of the head.

Pile Fabric A fabric with cut or whole loops that stand up on the surface, as in velvet, corduroy, and terry cloth.

Pillbox A small, round brimless hat with a flat tip and a cylindrical side.

Poke Bonnet A bonnet with a small crown at the back and a wide front brim which projects up and out from the face.

Pork Pie A snap-brimmed hat with the center of the crown pressed down and creased all around. It was first made popular in the mid-19th century, then during the 1940s.

Profile Hat A hat worn down over the side of the head to outline the wearer's face.

Puritan A somber black felt hat with a high, conical crown and a narrow straight brim. It was worn by Puritans in the 17th century and was usually trimmed with a front buckle.

Ribbon Wire Ribbon of crinoline or buckram, stiffened with one or two wires running through the middle.

Selvage The finished, lengthwise edges of woven fabric.

Shirring Stitch A series of short, parallel stitches that when pulled through create a gathered effect in the fabric.

Side Band The part of the crown that joins the brim.

Sisal A smooth, yellow straw with a linen finish that is made from Manila hemp.

Sizing Stiffeners made of millinery gelatin and water which are used to harden fabric and straw.

Skull Cap A close-fitting cap that covers only the crown of the head.

Slip Stitch A loose stitch used for sewing the headsize band around the crown. It is generally concealed between two thickness of fabric.

Slouch Hat A soft hat with high crown and flopping flexible brim. Sometimes called the "Garbo hat," after the well-known actress.

Snap Brim A hat with a medium crown and brim, such as the fedora, which can be bent into various positions.

Snood A hair net used to contain the hair at the back of the head.

Sombrero A hat made of either felt or straw with a tall crown and a very wide brim. Traditionally worn in Mexico and South America, the sombrero can be plain, or highly decorated with jewels and ribbon work.

Stovepipe A 19th-century top hat with a tall, cylindrical crown popularized by U.S. President Abraham Lincoln.

Straw Braid Braided straw used for sewing complete hats or as a trim. It is available in various widths and can be made of natural straw, imitation straw, or combinations of straw and yarn.

Swirling The shaping of millinery ribbon by stretching and shrinking its edges until a curve is formed.

Tam-o' Shanter A Scottish cap with a tight-fitting headband, a flat, round top, and a pompon in the center.

Ten-Gallon Hat A broad brim hat with a high, tapered crown worn by American cowboys.

Tie Tack A stitch used for attaching trimmings to a hat.

Topstitch A decorative stitch on brimmed hats.

Tie Wire Fine, uncovered wire used in trimming work.

Toque A small, brimless, fitted hat.

Toyo Cellophane-coated rice paper woven into a thin, shiny straw.

Tricorn A soft hat with a medium crown with the brim turned up on three sides.

Tulle Fine rayon, silk, or nylon net (also maline or illusion).

Turban A hat made from a long strip of cloth or a scarf worn coiled around the head.

Tuscan Fine, light yellow straw woven from the tops of wheat stalks.

Veil Thin, translucent net material worn as a hat ornament or to protect or hide the face (also called veiling).

Velvet Fabric with a short, soft, thick pile made from silk or silk/rayon blends.

Velveteen Imitates velvet in feel and texture but made of cotton or rayon.

Velour A hat finish where the nap is clipped to give a soft, raised velvety feel and look.

Viscas Artificial fibers woven to resemble straw.

Visor A partial brim extending out from the front of a hat or cap (also called peak).

Warp In woven fabric, the yarn running lengthwise, crossed at right angles to the weft.

Weft Horizontal filling yarn interlaced at a right angle through the warp, from selvage edge to selvage edge.

Whimsy A small piece of veil strip shaped to cover the head and part of the face.

Widow's Peak A close-fitting cap with a point coming down over the center of the forehead. Originally worn as a mourning bonnet by Catherine de Médicis.

Willow A woven and sized material made of esparto grass and cotton. It is used in making frames for expensive hats. It is also called esparterie or spartre. Not commonly available, it is best substituted by buckram.

Wimple A light piece of fabric framing the face and chin. Worn by women in medieval times, wimples regained popularity in the 1940s.

SOURCES

Many of the supplies used to make hats can be found in sewing stores, craft shops, and hardware stores. Specialty materials such as feathers, foundation materials, millinery ribbon, and millinery wire can be more difficult to find. You might look under hats or millinery supplies in your local business phone directory or search the Internet. In case you can't find the materials locally, here's a selection of mail-order suppliers.

NORTH AMERICA

Art Station LTD
144W 27th Street
NY, NY 10001
212- 807-8000
French curve #17, item # 1010-17

California Millinery Supply Co.
721 South Spring Street
Los Angeles, CA 90014
213-622-8746
Call for catalog

Cinderella Flower & Feather
60 West 38th St.
NY, NY 10018
212-840-0644
Flowers, veiling, rheinstones

Dersch Feathers
62 West 36th St.
NY, NY 10018
212-714-2806
Feathers

Dressmakers' Supply Co. Ltd
1212 Yonge St.
Toronto Ontario, Canada M4T 1W1
416-922-6000
Some millinery supplies, threads, beads, trims
$5 catalog

Hat Life Directory & Newsletter
66 York Street
Jersey City, NJ 07302
201-434-8322
Call for subscription rates

Hats by Leko
2081 Buffalo St.
Casper, WY 82604
1-800-817-HATS
Millinery supplies and trims
Call for catalog

Headquarters International Inc.
42 West 39th St.
NY, NY 10018
212-840-0990
Straw and horsehair braid

Holywood Fancy Feathers Co.
12140 Sherman Way North
Hollywood, CA 91605
818-765-1767 and 800-828-6689
Feathers
Free color brochure

Hyman Hendler & Sons
67 West 38th Street
NY, NY 10018
212-840- 8393
Spectacular imported novelty ribbons

Jiffy Steamer Co.
P.O. Box 869,
Union City, TN 38281
901-885-6690
Call for information about model J-1

Lacis
3163 Adeline Street
Berkeley, CA 94703
510-843-7178
Some foundation materials, wire, basic notions, artificial flowers and leaves
Call for a catalog

LaMode West
8470 Galpin Boulevard
Chanhassen, MN 55317
612-470-1907
Balsa and wood hat blocks

Log Cabin Dry Goods
E3445 French Gulch Road
Coeur d'Alene, ID 83814
208-664-5908
Timtex™ Interfacing

M&J Trimming
1008 6th Ave
NY, NY 10009
212-391-9072
Ribbons, rheinstones, beads, strung pearls

Manny's Millinery
26 W 38th Street
NY, NY 10018
212 840 2235/6
Buckram, flexie, flalene, French elastic, felt, straw, feathers, flowers, wire, and more.
Catalog $3

Millinery Supplies Co.
911 Elm
Dallas TX 75202
214-742-8284
Home page: www.milliners.com

Talas
568 Broadway
NY, NY 10012
212-219-0770
Acid-free tissue and boxes
Call for catalog and price list

Tinsel Trading
47 weat 38 st.
NYC 10018
212-730-1030
Vintage tassles, braids, trims

Henry Westfal & Co.
105 West 30th st.
NYC 10018
212-563-5990
Feather knives

SOURCES (cont.)

NORTH AMERICA (cont.)

Vogue Die Corp.
225 Norman Avenue
Brooklyn, NY 11222
718-383-5800
Electric hat stretcher

Eskay Novelty Co.
34 West 38th St.
New York, NY 10018
212-391-4110
Feathers

Zeeman's Corp.
270 West 38th Street
NY, NY 10018
212-302-2822
*Wire, 50-yard ribbon roll, #690 buckram, two-ply
buckram, flexie, flalean, French elastic, Rice's
Silamide thread, wire, needles*

OVERSEAS

MacCulloch & Wallis (London) Ltd
PO Box 3AX
25-26 Dering Street
London WIA 3AX, England
0171-409-0725
*Wire, buckram, millinery ribbons, beads,
sewing supplies*
f2 catalog along with A4 size SASE

The Hat Trade
Unit 3, Wealden/Beacon Business Park
Farmingham Road
Crowborough
East Sussex TN6 2JR, England
01892-667949
Millinery foundation materials, notions and wire
Call for catalog

PROFESSIONAL ASSOCIATIONS

Headwear Information Bureau
302 West 12th St.
New York, NY 10014
212-627-8333

The Millinery Arts Alliance
P.O. Box 577277
Chicago, IL 60657
312-409-6311

SUGGESTED READING

GENERAL INTEREST

Ginsburg, Madeleine. *The Hat, Trends and Traditions.* New York: Barron's, 1990.

Munker, Donna. *How to Wear Hats with Style.* New York: Crown Publishers, Inc., 1988.

Shields, Jody. Hats, *A Stylish History and Collector's Guide.* New York: Clarkson Potter, 1991.

Smith, Rodney, and Smolan, Leslie. *The Hat Book.* New York: Doubleday, 1993.

The editors of Victoria Magazine. *The Romance of Hats.* New York: Hearst Books, 1994.

RIBBON WORK

King, Candace. *The Artful Ribbon.* Lafayette, CA: C&T Publishing, 1996.

Kingdom, Christine. *Glorious Ribbons.* Radnor, PA: Chilton Book Company, 1993.

Picken, Nancy Brooks. *Old Fashioned Ribbon Trimmings and Flowers.* New York: Dover Publications, Inc., 1993.

Wolff, Colette. *The Art of Manipulating Fabric.* Radnor, PA: Chilton Book Co., 1996.

Ribbon Trimming, A Course in Six Parts. California: Sloane Publications, (reprint by Viv's Ribbon and Laces), 1992.

INDEX

A

Abbreviations, key to, 49
Adhesives
    for fabrics, 45
    for trims, 45
    Fusibles, 45
Anatomy
    of a hat, 49
    of a millinery feather,
      116

B

Balance and proportion, 50
Berets
    Multi-section, 66-68
    Photos of, 9, 11, 12, 20, 21
    Shirred, 54-56
    Stylized
        Four-section, 63
        Pagoda, 62
        Flat tip, 64
    Two-section, 57-59
Bias, true, 49
Blocking
    Cloches, 75, 76
    Simple crowns, 92, 93
Boaters
    How to make, 83-87
    Photos of, 10, 23, 24
Bows
    Fabric, 110
    S bow, 110
    Tailored, 109
Buckram, 41, 47

C

Cape net, 42, 47
Cloches
    How to make, 72-78
    Photos of, 18, 19
Cocktail caps
    How to keep them on, 104,
    105
    How to make, 102, 103,
    106, 107
    Photos of, 30-33
Combs, 104
Covering frames
    Pillbox, 82
    Boater, 86, 87
    Stylized brim, 88-91

D

Drafts, truing, 49
Draping, 97, 99
Dyeing
    Feathers, 118
    Silk flowers, 114

E

Elastic cord, tubular, 104
Equipment and materials, 41-45

F

Fabrics, choosing and handling,
    47, 48
Feather hats
    How to make
        Feather pads, 119
        One-by-one, 120-122
    Photos of, 34,-37
Feather knives, 118
Feathers
    Commercial categories,
    116, 117
    Handling, 118
    Pads, 116
    Storing, 118
    Trimming with
        Boa pompon, 123
        Coq-tail, 124
        Curled tail feather, 123
        Plumage rose, 122, 123
Figure 8 loop, 105
Flalean, 42
Flexible buckram (flexie), 41
Flowers
    Dyeing, 114
    Garlands of, 107
French curve, #17, 133
French elastic, 42, 47
French net, 42

G

Garlands
How to make, 107
Photos of, 29

H

Hat stretchers, 43
Headbands, 56, 58, 59
Headblocks, balsa, 44
Headsize plate, 45, 130, 131
Horsehair brims, 112, 115

I

Irons, 43

K

Keeping hats on, 104, 105

L

Linings
Materials, 42, 47, 48

M

Mail-order sources, 138-140
Markers, 45
Measuring tools, 43
Millinery needles, 44
Millinery ribbons, 50-52
Millinery ruler, 129
Millinery thread, 44
Millinery workroom setup, 126
Millinery workroom supplies, 126
Muslin, 42, 47

P

Pattern paper, 45
Pillboxes
How to make, 80-82
Photos of, 15, 16
Pins
pushpins, 45
straight pins, 45
Pliers, 44
Plumage, 117
Pressing roll, 43, 132
Pricing hats, 128

R

Ribbons
Grosgrain, 50, 51
Millinery, 50, 51
Rice's Silamide thread, 44

S

Scissors, 44
Sewing machines, 43
Simple blocked crowns, 92
Special occasion hats
How to make, 101-114
Photos of, 17
Starting a small business, 127, 128
Steamers, 43
Stitches
Back, 46
Basting, 46
Buttonhole, 46
Cross, 46
Overcast, 46
Pick, 46
Running, 46
Shirring, 46
Slip, 46
Tie, 46
Whip, 47
Straw braids, 86, 87
Sweatbands, inserting, 51, 52
Swirling ribbons, 51

T

Thimbles, 44
Trade shows, 128
Trimmings
Ribbons and bows, 109, 110
Rosettes, 111
Turbans
How to make
Basic, 95-97
Built-up, 98-100
Photos of, 13, 14

V

Veils, 112
Visors
How to make, 69-71
Photos of, 22

W

Wire
Frame wire, 42
Tie wire, 43
Steel wire, 42